ACES FULL

By Robert Grinsell

Robert 'Bob' Grinsell is a 1960 graduate of the University of Santa Clara with a B.A. Degree in Mechanical Engineering. Following graduation he joined Aerojet where he has spent his entire 30 year professional career. Initially working as a Design Engineer, he presently is Vice President of Advanced Programs where he is responsible for Strategic Planning, Technology Development, and Advanced Program Acquisition for Aerojet Solid Propulsion.

An avid aviation historian, he devoted over five years of research, including extensive personal contact with pilots from throughout the world, to produce this colorful and accurate document of the aces who fought World War II.

SBN 913194-03-4

GenCorp
Aerojet

ACKNOWLEDGEMENTS

I wish to take this opportunity and space to express my sincere and heartfelt appreciation to all the individuals and organizations whose interest and cooperation have made this series a reality. My deepest gratitude is extended to: Captain D.R. Aggers and the staff of the United States Marine Corps Division of Information; Carroll Anderson; Major Larry Brown and the staff of the United States Air Force Division of Information; Garry Fry; General Services Administration; Imperial War Museum; Yasuho Izawa; Mrs. Tateo Kato; Mrs. Teruhiko Kobayashi; Philip Markham; Wayne McCorrister; Lt. Commander R.D. McEwen, Anna Urband, Robert Carlisle and the staff of the United States Navy Information Office; The Royal Air Force; Peter Robertson and the staff of the Historical Photographs Section of the Public Archives of Canada; Christopher Shores; Takehura Shimanuki, Chief, Japanese War History Unit; Dwayne Tabatt; Doug Tidy; Raymond Toliver; The West German Air Force; S.F. Wise and the staff of the Directorate of History, Canadian Armed Forces; the combat aces themselves, and, most of all my wife and family, whose patience and belief in my project has never dimmed in the face of my many late hours and long days which could just as easily have been spent with them.

INTRODUCTION

Aces Full is a new series of aviation books which present a compilation of biographical information, photographs and illustrations on the outstanding World War II combat fighter pilots and their aircraft. These aces are listed in alphabetical order including their country, units, and their total credited victories. The victory credits are official credited aerial kills and do not include ground victories. Although various Allied units did allow their pilots to display ground victories on their planes and to include them in their total count, the Credit Boards of all nations recognized only confirmed air victories in establishing their aces. The commonly accepted necessary number of enemy aircraft destroyed to reach ace status was five, although some countries, like Germany, set much higher plateaus for their pilots' decorations. Of the many thousands of pilots who flew in World War II, a relatively few were to attain the status of ace.

The information contained in this, and subsequent volumes, has been researched from official records, photographs, correspondence, and personal contacts. However, due to the time span between these events and the present, the sometimes hurried manner with which some of the combat information was recorded during the war years, and the variation in aircraft paint tones due to weathering, light intensity and photographic processing differences, the author cannot say with absolute certainty that the contents of this book are not subject to slight conjecture.

Also, there still exist, several areas where data is not available and this results in the fact that some details will never be fully clarified. One such area is the total confirmed victories of several Royal Air Force and Japanese pilots. The reasons behind this phenomenon are simple, and yet, unfortunately, for the historian, irrevocable. During many of the combat actions of World War II, the expediency of staying alive or defending a given strategic location did not allow time for detailed record keeping and on occasion when it did, these records were often times destroyed prior to occupation by the opposing forces. Thus, without confirmation, many victories will remain unclaimed and forgotten. In the case of the Japanese pilots, the added influence of the Asian code of rank and honor added to the existing confusion. It was often frowned upon for lesser ranks to have more victories than the commanding officers, and thus, it was customary to award victories achieved by Japanese pilots to the aircraft they were flying that day or to their unit rather than to the pilot himself. Much information has been researched to clarify some of these victories, but just as certain, many excellent pilots will never receive the full credit that is due them.

It is the hope of the author that this series of books will serve as authentic reference material for all those interested in the colorful aviation history which was created and lived by the combat fighter pilot of WW II.

FOREWORD

BY BRIGADIER GENERAL ROBIN OLDS, RET.

Here is a book without a plot, a tale without a beginning, a story without an end. There is not one paragraph describing the background, not one word of conversation, not one line of character development. There is no formulation of purpose, no definition of conflict, no delineation of emotional involvement, no measure of stress, of tension, of hate, of love or fear.

Yet of action there is abundance, and of central characters a-plenty. Here you will find individuals, each playing his part against a background drama of intense conflict, each driven by an inner compulsion to excel, and each buoyed and sustained by a unique combination of skill, emotional drive, mental agility, and courage.

You, the reader, must fill in the background, drawing the panoply of war from the recesses of memory or imagination, and filling the void of personal contention with your own definitions of right and wrong, good and bad.

There is something else you must do. Something you must appreciate about the men who fill these pages. It is something that may be sensed, but can scarcely be understood except by the men themselves and others like them. If you have ever hunted dangerous big game alone, depending upon your own wits and skill for success, then you have a glimmering. If you ever found yourself the hunted, not the hunter, then your glimmering is increased. If you can imagine the animal you hunted, or were hunted by, had the advantage of human intelligence as well as an ability to kill equal to your own, your glimmering of understanding is now knowledge. Think of this as you read the exploits of these men.

Think too of the environment in which they fought, and of the machines created to do their bidding. Unlike any other aircraft, the fighter operates in a truly three dimensional arena. During air-to-air combat, *up* is limited only by the function of power, *down* by the surface of the earth, *around* by structural strength of the aircraft and the physical condition of the pilot. Right-side-up and up-side-down have relevance only to the opponent. Your position with respect to him (and a very healthy vice-versa) is the only thing important at any given second. Realize that the successful fighter pilot projects ahead in time. He thinks and reacts in terms of the positions and relative displacements he wishes to reach seconds to minutes ahead of *now*. He must also do this for his opponent — gauging the total options available to the enemy, calculating relative speeds, "G" forces, angles, — anticipating moves — in short, striving to think and fly as though he were in both cockpits.

In aerial engagements involving more than two aircraft, the problem is complicated geometrically. To the best of his ability, the fighter pilot must keep track of the relative position and inherent threat of every aircraft in the fight, friend and foe alike, for a mid-air collision is totally impartial, and the enemy you don't see is always the one that will get you. This means that you must do everything in your power not just to see, but more important, to assess movements and project relative positions. And all the while, if you are in a position of command, you must gauge the entire battle situation and instruct your own people accordingly. It takes skill and experience to do this, skill developed by hours of practice, experience gained in your first few fights. After a while action and reaction become almost instinctive. You are scarcely aware of the rapid thought processes — considering, rejecting, deciding, acting. Often you make a mistake and if you live, you learn. You find yourself going over and over every moment, every detail of every fight in the quiet before sleep. You read every report. You pump every friend. You study every conceivable situation that might occur in a future battle. You plot and plan and, in between times, no matter how weary, you use the time during return from a mission to train yourself and your people. The payoff comes that day when you have anticipated the enemy and he is there, where you knew he would be, doing what you knew he would be doing at that time and place. You hit him hard, force the fight, bend him to your will, scatter him to the winds, cut him into small pieces, and attack, attack, attack!

Sometimes it's not that way and the smart leader obeys the dictates of prudence, instinct and experience telling him to break off, the odds are stacked. You'll come back tomorrow, wiser from the experience — and you'll fight again.

There are fighter pilots and there are fighter pilots. Only a few achieve total mastery. The combination of skill, desire, and opportunity is rare. But for those recognized in this volume, the ingredients were there and they fought their way to recognition in an exclusive fraternity, the brotherhood of Fighter Aces.

Don't be surprised to learn that these men hold each other in deep respect, a respect that crosses the borders of nations and transcends the bounds of political ideology. Old hatreds fade. The common bond of shared experience, of violent action, of exhilarating success, and of numbing failure is all that counts. Yet should the demand be made, not one of these old war horses would fail to respond to the call again.

Younger men have taken over. Conflict continues and will continue as long as man exists. New pages of accomplishment and bravery are being written in slashing aerial battle. And in some distant day, people will look back upon these pilots and will see in them the courage and the heart that has led mankind from the caves toward the stars.

TABLE OF CONTENTS

THE ACES Page

ANDERSON, Major Clarence E.
United States Army Air Force
363rd Fighter Sqdn.
8th Air Force
(16.25 Victories)

Born on January 13, 1922 in Oakland, California, Anderson attended and graduated from Placer Union High School and then went on to Sacramento Junior College where he graduated in 1941. He learned to fly in the Civilian Pilot Training Program (CPTP) while in Sacramento, soloing and receiving his private license in late 1941. Shortly after the Japanese attack on Pearl Harbor, Anderson volunteered for Air Cadet pilot training and was posted to Williams Field in Arizona for his pre-flight training. From there he was sent to the Ryan School in San Diego, California piloting PT-22s as part of his primary training, received his basic flight training at Minter Field, Bakersfield, California in BT-13s and was then sent to Luke Field, Arizona where he transitioned into the AT-6 and received his wings and a commission as a second lieutenant on September 29, 1942.

Assigned to the 328th Fighter Group at Hamilton Field, California and Oakland Municipal Airport, he stayed for six months before transferring to the 363rd Fighter Squadron, 357th Fighter Group, a newly formed unit flying the Bell P-39 Airacobra. The unit moved to several locations before finally being sent overseas, in November 1943. Based at Leiston, England with their new North American P-51 Mustangs, with Anderson as a Flight Commander, they were the first 8th Air Force unit to receive the new fighter.

The unit started combat operations on February 8, 1944 flying a fighter escort mission to Frankfurt, Germany. Anderson's first combat claim occurred two weeks later when during another escort mission to Leipzig, he damaged an attacking Fw 190. His first victory was achieved on March 8th when he destroyed a Me 109 northwest of Hanover while escorting Allied bombers on a raid to Berlin. A month later, on April 11th, he scored his second victory in nearly the same location, again downing a Me 109 and during the same mission was credited with sharing in the destruction of a He 111 with three other pilots of the 363rd. For the rest of the month, Anderson flew almost continuous escort and fighter sweep sorties into France and Germany, but didn't score again until the 30th when he shot down a Fw 190 southeast of Orleans during an escort mission. A week later on May 8th, he accounted for his fourth victory when he destroyed another Fw 190, this time over Soltau. Anderson reached ace status on May 12th, just northeast of Frankfurt, when he destroyed his third Me 109 during an escort mission to Brux, Czechoslovakia.

Anderson's next victories were scored on May 27th northwest of Strasbourg, France. "We were escorting bombers to the Ludwigshafen-Mannheim area on May 27, 1944. We were flying a group formation with my squadron on the right flank, and as we rendezvoused with the B-17s at around 27,000 feet, we crossed over the bombers and started to make a lazy turn to the left. The group leader identified our bombers and then immediately someone called over the R/T that there was a large number of enemy fighters about to attack the bomber formation immediately in front of ours.

"We released our drop tanks and turned sharp left to engage the fighters. At this point the flight I was leading was placed on the outside of the turn, and was therefore vulnerable to attack from the rear. Before I could look behind, my element leader, First Lieutenant Edward K. Simpson Jr. of Hampton, New Jersey, called out that four Me-109s were diving on our tails from five o'clock high.

"My flight turned sharply into the Me-109s as we fell into a close string formation. The lead German was a sharp customer, but his attack was thwarted by our sharp turn, so the four Germans pulled up and began circling with us.

"At full throttle and rpm we were able to maintain our turn inside them. Climbing to 29,000 feet we caught them and began to gain a little on each turn. Thereupon, the Germans decided to try something else. Turning east, three of them flew level at 29,000 while the number four man climbed as quickly as possible in the same direction.

"Lieutenant Simpson and his wingman pursued the climbing Me 109. With my wingman, I continued to chase the other three enemy aircraft. They were at full throttle as we could see the black exhaust pouring from their engines. Our own throttles were clear to the firewalls, and we slowly crept behind the last German. Holding my fire until about 250 yards dead astern, I fired a short burst and got some good hits around the wing roots and fuselage.

"More black smoke began to pour from his aircraft, only this time it wasn't exhaust. He rolled over on his back and flew upside down in an attempt to shake me, but I stayed level and fired another close-range burst. Chunks flew off and he burst into flames and began spinning lazily down to the deck.

"We now closed in on the two remaining Germans. The leader pulled up sharply into a climbing turn, and his wingman rolled over and went diving for home. We cut across the leading German's climbing circle, which he tightened, and I was forced to pull up

sharply to avoid colliding, because he now reversed his turn and was pulling his nose up for a shot at my wingman, Lieutenant Skara. Skara immediately threw his Mustang into a spin to avoid being hit, and as he descended the Me-109 followed him down. I followed.

"As I closed the range, the German broke violently into a climbing left turn and I had to pull up sharply again, whereupon the German reversed his turn, pulling up steeply for a short burst at me. He was very close, and I could see the detail and color of his highly polished aircraft. Luckily, he couldn't get his nose high enough to get a clean shot. He stalled just before I did and as we both nosed down to gain speed I was again behind him.

"Once more he pulled up into his tight left climbing turn. This time I throttled back slightly and stayed inside his turn. He saw that I wasn't going to overshoot him this time and he pulled almost straight up. Following, I was able to get in a long burst which connected in his cockpit and engine. He burst into flames and smoke, rolled slightly and then dove straight for the earth from 30,000 feet.

"I joined up with my wingman and went home, where we learned that Lieutenant Simpson had destroyed the fourth German, with the pilot bailing out at 20,000 feet. The group had engaged the main enemy fighter attack, destroying twenty-three of them."

Anderson was credited with another Me 109 on May 30th east of Schonebeck and on June 29th destroyed three Fw 190s southwest of Leipzig while on bomber escort duty to run his total score to 11.25. A week later the bombers returned to Leipzig and Anderson and the 363rd were again assigned escort duty. On this mission he shot down a Me 109 just north of the target area. He flew two more missions, both escort to Reims and Munich before he was given leave on July 12, 1944 and returned home to the United States.

Anderson returned to combat duty with the 357th Fighter Group in October 1944 flying the first sortie of his second tour on October 5th. His first score of that second tour occurred on November 27th during a fighter sweep and strafing mission to Annaburg when he was credited with the destruction of two Fw 190s northwest of Nordhausen. He also was credited with a probable during this mission. His final tallies were achieved on December 5th while on escort operation with B-17s over Berlin. On this day Anderson again destroyed a pair of Fw 190s over the city, and was also credited with another probable. This brought his final score to 16.25 aerial victories, 1 ground victory, 2 probables, and 2 damaged, his best day coming on June 29, 1944 when he shot down three Fw 190s over Leipzig, during a long range penetration mission.

Anderson completed his second tour on February 1, 1945 and returned to the United States where he was assigned to Perrin Field, Texas as the Group Commander of the training command there. He remained there until the war's end. In all, he flew over 480 operational hours with the 357th Fighter Group and was decorated with the Distinguished Flying Cross and four oak leaf clusters, the Air Medal with thirteen oak leaf clusters, and the French Croix de Guerre. The P-51 Mustang he piloted with the 363rd Fighter Squadron, 357th Fighter Group in the late autumn of 1944 is illustrated on page 59.

Major Clarence Anderson's P-51D-10-NA (S/N 44-14450) "Old Crow", Powerplant: one 1,490 hp. V-1650-7 engine. Top speed: 437 mph. at 25,000 ft. Cruise speed: 362 mph. Armament: six .50 caliber machine guns. Range: 950 miles.

BACCUS, Lt. Colonel Donald A.
359th Fighter Squadron
356th Fighter Group
8th Air Force
(5 Victories)

Donald Arthur Baccus, born on May 29, 1916, attended Concordia College in Moorehead, Minnesota from 1934 through 1936 at which time he quit school with the intention of entering the Army Aviation Cadet Program (two years of college level instruction were necessary to qualify). However, during this time, Baccus noticed his eyesight beginning to blur and, after an examination, was fitted with glasses which dampened any hopes he had of qualifying for pilot training. Moving to Los Angeles, California, in 1937, Baccus worked at odd jobs until early in 1940 when, by accident, his glasses were broken and without the funds to purchase a new pair, he found that his eyes had seemingly returned to normal. In April he took his Army physical and was qualified for pilot training.

Baccus was sent to Oxnard, California, where he completed his primary training, then to Randolph Field for basic flight training, and on to Kelly Field, Texas for his advanced training where he graduated in March 1941. Assigned to Randolph Field as a flight instructor, he remained there until October, at which time he was transferred to Foster Field, Victoria, Texas as an instructor pilot in AT-6s. In late 1942, Baccus, still under the direct command of Foster Field, moved to Matagorda Island off the Texas coast to command the Gunnery School.

April 1942, found him at Westover, Massachusetts checking out in the Republic P-47B Thunderbolt, and on the 23rd he became part of the 322nd Fighter Squadron, 326th Fighter Group. In July he was transferred from the 326th Fighter Group to the 356th Fighter Group as the C.O. of the 359th Fighter Squadron at Grenier Field, New Hampshire. The 356th was at this time preparing for assignment in the United Kingdom and plans called for the entire unit to fly over. However, at the last moment, the aircraft and personnel boarded ships. Arriving in England in late August, the 356th spent the first two months at Goxhill, before being permanently assigned to RAF Martlesham Heath in early October.

Baccus flew his first combat mission on October 15th, but the flight proved uneventful. He was credited with his first victory a month later when he destroyed a Me 109 while on bomber escort duty in a P-47D-5. Between December 1943 and mid-November 1944, Baccus continued flying the P-47D and was credited with one additional aerial victory and three enemy aircraft destroyed on the ground. During November the 359th transitioned to the North American P-51D Mustang, and on the 26th, Baccus, piloting one of the new planes, was credited with his only

Hard landing! This P-51D from 356th Fighter Group flipped over in the Belgian snow during Battle of the Bulge. Mustang bears same checkerboard cowl pattern as that flown by Col. Baccus.

multiple victory day.

It was one of the first all-out missions in which the unit flew the new aircraft. They were assigned as escorts to the lead formation of B-17s on a raid in the Hanover area. Receiving radio verfication of Luftwaffe aircraft ahead at an altitude of 24,000 feet, Baccus left one Squadron for protection of the bombers and led the remaining two squadrons to intercept the German fighters. Approaching at 26,000 feet, Baccus destroyed two Me 109s on his first pass and the unit was credited with a total of twenty-six without the loss of a single pilot. This mission proved a real morale builder for the 356th, as up until this time they had been somewhat unsure about their new planes, having trained and fought for over a year in the rugged P-47.

On November 3rd, Baccus temporarily assumed command of the entire 356th Fighter Group. He remained in this position until January 10, 1945, when the commanding officer, Colonel Philip E. Tukey returned from leave.

On April 1st, Baccus was transferred from the 356th Fighter Group to the 359th Fighter Group as Commanding Officer, a position he held until the end of hostilities.

Baccus finished the war with five confirmed aerial victories (all Me 109s) and three ground victories and was decorated with the Silver Star, the Distinguished Flying Cross, with two oak leaf clusters and the Air Medal with ten oak leaf clusters. He flew over 125 combat missions and logged more than 400 combat hours. The P-51D-15 piloted by Baccus during November 1944 with the 359th Fighter Squadron and one of the P-51s he flew while commanding the 359th Fighter Group in mid-1945 are illustrated on page 58.

P-51s line up at English base after close of hostilities in Germany.

BATZ, Major Wilhelm
Fighter Wing 52 (JG 52)
Luftwaffe
(237 Victories)

Wilhelm "Willi" Batz, born in Bamberg, Bavaria on May 21, 1916, enlisted in the prewar Luftwaffe in 1935, and after completion of his pilot training was assigned to instructor duty. Even after the beginning of hostilities, his unique abilities to teach young fighter pilots kept him in training positions although he constantly applied for a transfer to a combat unit. Finally, in December of 1942, Batz was posted to II/JG 52 in Russia as Adjutant to Johannes Steinhoff, the Group Commander. Although Batz took to the air on combat sorties at every opportunity, after over four months of flying, he had not accounted for a single Soviet aircraft. Dejected, and convinced he would never become a fighter ace, he asked for a transfer to the Luftwaffe Bomber Command. His request, however, was denied, and on March 11, 1943 Batz was credited with his first victory.

In May, Batz was promoted to command one of the Group's squadrons. Ironically he was probably the only *Staffel Kapitän* who was not an air ace on the Russian Front, but his score started to rise slowly, and by January 1944 it stood at fifteen. The following month, Batz became ill and was taken off flying status for a two week period. Upon his return to duty, he began the most incredible string of aerial kills of the war. Throughout the spring and summer months, he found plenty of Soviet aircraft activity in JG 52's area, and was consistently credited with three and four planes a day. As his score increased, so did his fame, and as was the case with almost all high scoring Luftwaffe aces on the Russian Front, he became a prime target for the Russian sharpshooters. On several occasions, Batz was singled out by the Soviet pilots, however, in each instance his luck and flying skill was enough to insure his escape, although, physical wounds and aircraft damage became ever present companions. On six separate occasions, Batz forcelanded his Me 109s, and he soon took to flying aircraft practically devoid of personal markings, the traditional kill wreaths and scrolls on the rudder being eliminated.

Between February and the end of March 1944, Batz raised his victory total to the century level, and then, in a phenomenal rash of victories, destroyed his 200th enemy plane by August 17th. Included in these victories were an incredible fifteen scored on May 30th on seven separate missions, and sixteen on a day in mid-August. Only two other Luftwaffe aces scored more confirmed victories in a single day. These were Hans-Joachim Marseille, seventeen on September 1, 1942 in North Africa, and Emil "Bully" Lang, eighteen on the Eastern Front.

Batz was given command of Third Group, Fighter Wing 52 (III/JG 52) in June 1944, relieving Günther Rall, after the latter had been transferred to the Western Front. Under his command were pilots the likes of Erich Hartmann (352 victories) and Walter Wolfrum (137 victories). It is no doubt that the competition that existed among the pilots in his *Gruppe*, aided Batz both as a commander and as a fighter pilot. He remained in command of this unit until January 2, 1945, when he assumed command of II/JG 52 in Hungary, replacing Gerhard Barkhorn, who was assigned to the new Me 262 under the command of Adolf Galland.

The new command proved to be a stroke of good fortune for Batz, as with the end of the war in sight, he was able to lead his unit from Hungary, through Austria, and into Germany where he surrendered them to the advancing American Forces rather than to the Soviet Forces on the Eastern borders. This move enabled Batz and his unit to avoid the imprisonment and torture that befell the other two *Gruppes* and Staff of JG 52.

Batz ended the war with a total of 237 confirmed aerial victories, only five of which were scored against the Western Powers. He was decorated with the Knights Cross on March 26, 1944, the Oak Leaves on July 20, 1944 and the Swords on April 21, 1945. Batz flew over 440 combat missions in the Me 109 and was wounded three times. He ranked as the Luftwaffe's sixth highest scoring fighter ace and his 220 victories in a single year is a record not likely to be equalled.

The Me 109G piloted by Batz as Adjutant to Johannes Steinhoff with II/JG 52 in late 1942 and early 1943 is illustrated on page 34.

While his students went off to war, Wilhelm Batz continued to train pilots in the Me 109 for the first three years of the war. It was not until March of 1943 that he was credited with his initial victory. But Batz learned quickly and within 17 months had reached the 200 victory mark.

BEURLING, Flt. Lieutenant George F.
403 Squadron
Royal Canadian Air Force
(31 Victories)

George Frederick "Screwball" Beurling, born in Verdun, a suburb of Montreal, Canada, on December 6, 1921 grew up fascinated with flying. He spent his spare money on flying lessons and when war broke out, volunteered as a pilot but was denied because of his lack of educational qualifications although he had passed both written and flying exams. He then volunteered for the Finnish Air Force and was accepted, but because of his age, his father refused to give consent. Beurling continued to fly, concentrating his efforts on academics. In May 1940 he sailed to England and volunteered for the Royal Air Force. On September 7th he was finally accepted for pilot training.

Beurling spent over a year in fighter training before winning his wings on September 9, 1941. He was then posted to 403 Squadron (RCAF) where he took part in his first combat operations flying fighter sweeps over the English Channel and on into Northern France from October 1941 through May 1942. It was with this unit he accounted for his first victory when on May 1st he destroyed a Fw 190 over Calais.Two days later he shot down another Fw 190 for what proved to be his final victory in this area, as in June, Beurling was transferred to 249 Squadron based at Takali on Malta.

Beurling flew his first combat with 249 Squadron on June 12th when he and three other pilots from the unit engaged a formation of Luftwaffe Me 109s which were strafing the RAF airfields on the island. Although no victories were achieved by either side, Beurling was credited with damaging one of the intruders before they broke off contact and headed back to their base in Sicily. The following month, inclement weather over Malta allowed the embittered defenders to enjoy a much needed rest from the constant bombing and harassment of the Luftwaffe and *Regia Aeronautica*, but on July 6th the weather cleared and the enemy raids began once again. Early that morning, Beurling and seven other 249 pilots took off to intercept a formation of Italian bombers and escorting fighters heading for Luqa. On sighting the enemy, Beurling selected one of the leading fighters and attacked with cannon and machine guns. He flew by his first target and immediately climbed to engage a Macchi 202 which he quickly sent flaming into the sea below. He turned back into the enemy formation and destroyed a second Macchi 202 before being forced to return to Takali to refuel and rearm. Beurling took off again, this time being directed to a pair of Luftwaffe Me 109s heading toward Malta. As the aircraft closed, the 109s split up and tried to climb away from Beurling, but he picked out one of the enemy and opened fire. The Me 109 started to trail a steady stream of smoke, turned over, on its side, and dove directly into the Mediterranean. That brought Beurling's one day score to three, and made him an ace.

The following day Beurling was in the air again, this time to intercept a flight of four Ju 88s which were escorted by over twenty Me 109s. Beurling ignored the slower bombers and headed into the escort formation where he sighted one of the enemy on the tail of a Spitfire. He pulled up under the Me 109's tail and fired into its undersurface. The enemy plane did a complete roll, burst into flames and spun into the water. Later the same day he accounted for victory number seven when he destroyed a Macchi 202 while on patrol. On the 11th, Beurling again was vectored to intercept an incoming bomber and escort formation and in the ensuing mixup was credited with another Macchi 202. Two hours later, he and another pilot from 249 Squadron were on the day's second patrol when they sighted two Macchi 202s apparently heading home across the sea. Beurling caught up with the rearmost aircraft and opened fire. He watched it as the pilot bailed out and the plane crashed into the Mediterranean. Beurling next banked his Spitfire around and, with his wingman flying cover, attacked the second enemy plane. It joined its partner in the sea below. Beurling had now accounted for ten enemy aircraft, eight of which had been destroyed in just three days of fighting over Malta.

On July 27th, the squadron intercepted another formation of Ju 88s and escorting 202s and 109s. Beurling sighted a flight of four of the Italian planes and proceeded to attack the nearest of the enemy. It turned right into his deadly stream of fire in its efforts to evade the Canadian pilot. Beurling watched as it crash landed on the beach below. He then turned his attention to the other three Macchi 202s and methodically proceeded to destroy one of them, the second fighter exploding in mid-air, before Beurling broke off his attack to concentrate on a pair of Me 109s which had moved in below him. He put his Spitfire into a slow wide roll, pulled up beneath the Luftwaffe fighters and opened fire. Both of the enemy aircraft caught fire and were abandoned by their pilots.

During the months of August and September, the action over Malta took on an unexpected lull, as the Luftwaffe and *Regia Aeronautica* remained in Sicily to refit and heal the wounds they had absorbed in the continual fighting of the previous two months. Towards the end of September, the lull came to an end and Beurling went back into action. During October, Beurling saw only two days of operational flying, but during those two days added six Luftwaffe aircraft to his score to bring his total victory tally to 20. On the 13th, he took part in a patrol that was vectored to intercept a formation of over 100 Luftwaffe aircraft. After destroying two escorting Me 109s, Beurling turned his attention to the bombers and quickly disposed of one of them. The following day he repeated his feat by accounting for another pair of Me 109s and a Ju 88. However, Beurling himself was wounded by enemy fire and forced to bail out into the Mediterranean. After recovery from his wounds, he was posted to instructor duty where he remained until September 1943 when he was transferred to the RCAF and posted back to 403 Squadron. There, he destroyed one Fw 190 before he was transferred to 412 Squadron, where on December 30th he achieved his 31st and final victory, another Fw 190.

Developed to combat the Fw 190 which was outperforming the Spitfire V, the Spit IX was basically a Mk V airframe adapted to take the new Merlin 61 engine of 1,660 hp. Although an interim model, it was produced in greater quantities than any other, 5,665 of this type being manufactured. It was built with clipped, standard and extended winged versions. Shown here is a standard Mk IX equipped with a pair of 20mm cannon and a pair of .50 caliber machine guns.

BLAKESLEE, Colonel Donald J.M.
335th Fighter Squadron
4th Fighter Group
8th Air Force
(15 Victories)

Donald James Mathew Blakeslee, born at Fairport Harbor, Ohio, on September 11, 1917, was appointed a second lieutenant in the United States Army Reserve on October 5, 1938. He served in this capacity until September 13, 1940 when he requested and received an honorable discharge in order to enlist in the Royal Canadian Air Force. After completion of his Canadian flight training, he was sent to England, arriving in May 1941. Blakeslee was assigned to 401 "Ram" Squadron of the RCAF, flying Supermarine Spitfires from Biggin Hill. He flew with this unit for almost a year on fighter sweeps inside France and on bomber interception duty, gaining his first aerial kill, an Me 109, and being decorated with the British Distinguished Flying Cross. In early 1942, Blakeslee was reassigned with other American born pilots in Commonwealth units to 133 "Eagle" Squadron as a flight commander, and in August destroyed two Fw 190s to increase his score to three. In September 1942, Blakeslee and the other American volunteers of the three "Eagle" Squadrons (71, 121, and 133) were transferred to the 8th Air Force to become the nucleus of the 4th Fighter Group. Activated at Bushey Hall, headquarters of the 8th Air Forces Fighter Command, the squadrons officially became part of the USAAF on the 29th during formal ceremonies at Debden, England. From there, Blakeslee flew on the 4th's first combat mission, a fighter sweep into France on October 2, 1942.

He was then given command of the 335th Fighter Squadron, and in March the unit received Republic P-47Cs to replace the Spitfire Vs that they had brought with them when they were transferred into the 4th Fighter Group. Blakeslee became the first pilot in his unit to achieve a victory in the new plane, when on April 15, 1943 he destroyed a Fw 190 near Ostend, Belgium. Under Blakeslee's leadership the unit accounted for fifty enemy aircraft during the period between August and December 1943, with only minor losses to the 4th and the bomber units they escorted.

On January 1, 1944 Blakeslee assumed full command of the 4th Fighter Group with a total of nine victories to his credit, and on January 7th, while leading an escort mission for a bombing operation inside Germany, he achieved his tenth victory and was awarded the Distinguished Service Cross for his actions. The citation accompanying his decoration describes the events of that day:

Blakeslee's Spitfire V while assigned to 401 "Ram" Squadron, RCAF, Biggin Hill, summer and fall of 1941. It was in this aircraft that he scored his first kill, before being reassigned to 133 Eagle Squadron early in 1942.

"For extraordinary heroism in aerial combat over enemy territory in the vicinity of Hesdin, France. Colonel Blakeslee, on 7 January 1944, after engaging a flight of six enemy aircraft intent on the destruction of crippled and straggling heavy bombers, observed ten to twelve Fw 190s attacking unescorted bombers which were above him. Though attacked by three enemy aircraft from astern and flying into heavy and accurate fire which struck and damaged his aircraft, Colonel Blakeslee, disregarding damage, unfavorable altitude, obscured vision from spraying oil, and enemy superiority, climbed into the mass of enemy aircraft which he attacked and scattered, pursuing one of them through the haze to 2,000 feet, where he destroyed it before escape could be accomplished. Colonel Blakeslee's courage, aggressiveness, and will to destroy the enemy in the face of overwhelming odds reflect the greatest credit upon himself and the Armed Forces of the United States."

Between June 21st and July 5th Blakeslee led the 4th in a fighter escort protection mission to cover bombers in the first of the famed England to Russia shuttle bombing raids. On this unprecedented mission, Blakeslee overcame the obstacles of poor navigational facilities, adverse weather and enemy fighter opposition in such a manner that not a single loss was suffered by the bombers while under escort from the 4th Fighter Group. While sweeping in front of the bombers on the return mission over Budapest, Hungary on July 2, 1944, Blakeslee sighted over fifty enemy fighters and immediately led his flight of four aircraft to attack. Joined later by two other flights, the Americans routed the Luftwaffe fighters destroying 10 of them without loss to themselves. Blakeslee, himself, was credited with one of the enemy, his final victory of the war.

In September 1944, Blakeslee was given leave and rotated home to the United States. Returning to England in October, he was grounded because of his extensive air time and was sent back to the States for the remainder of the war. Considered by his peers as one of the finest all-around combat pilots and tacticians of World War II, Blakeslee's Group scored more victories than any other American unit in the ETO and he himself flew over 1000 combat hours. Although directly responsible for the planning and execution of most of the 4th's missions, he always managed to lead them on the "big ones". He finished the war with fifteen aerial victories and was credited with an additional six ground kills. He was decorated with the British Distinguished Flying Cross as well as the American Silver Star, the Distinguished Flying Cross, the Distinguished Service Cross and four Air Medals. A P-47 and one of the P-51s flown by Blakeslee while with the 4th Fighter Group are illustrated on page 45.

◀ P-51B was first Mustang flown by Blakeslee's 335th Fighter Sqdn., which together with the 334th, 336th and 337th, made up the famed 4th Fighter Gp. (Bodie Col.)

P-47C was first American fighter flown in combat by Blakeslee with brand new 4th Fighter Group. Prior to that, unit had operated Spit Vs from their old Eagle Squadron days. Blakeslee was first pilot to score with new Thunderbolt. ▶

CAREY, Group Captain Frank R.
43 Squadron
Royal Air Force
(28+ Victories)

Frank Reginald Carey, born in London, England on May 7, 1912, always knew he would someday be a fighter pilot. When he reached his fifteenth birthday, he joined the RAF as an apprentice at Halton Aircraft Apprentice School and spent three years receiving instruction in the maintenance of the latest fighter aircraft in RAF inventory. In 1930, after completion of his course, Carey was posted to 'A' Flight of 43 Squadron as a mechanic where he remained until 1934 at which time he was returned to Halton for advanced engineering training. From Halton he was sent to RAF Worthy Down and from there to No. 6 Flying Training School at Netheravon for flight instruction. In September 1935 Carey achieved his childhood dream, and was posted to 43 Squadron at Tangmere as a Sergeant Pilot.

Flying Hawker Hurricanes, the unit found little action against the Luftwaffe until January 1940 when Carey and his wingman intercepted a Heinkel 111 while on convoy protection patrol over the North Sea. The RAF fighters attacked the lone German bomber forcing it to jettison its load of bombs prematurely and head into cloud cover. Carey achieved several hits on the enemy plane before it reached the clouds, but no confirmation as to its destruction was reported. This was, however, the squadron's first claim of any kind and was welcome relief after long and monotonous months of nonproductive escort and patrol. It was also an omen of things to come. On February 12th the squadron was credited with their first victory in which Carey shared. He and another pilot were again on convoy patrol when the ships were attacked by a lone He 111. The Hurricanes did not miss this time, and Carey received credit for a shared kill.

On April 3rd Carey was reassigned to 3 Squadron in France as part of the air support for the British ground troops. On the first sortie he flew with the new unit he accounted for his first full victory, which was also the first victory for 3 Squadron. He had taken off with two other pilots in a fighter sweep near Merville when they sighted several He 111s below them. Carey singled out one of the bombers and opened fire sending it flaming to the ground below. He continued to attack the remaining bombers, but ran out of ammunition and was forced to return to his base to rearm and refuel. He took off again for his second patrol of the day and intercepted a formation of Do 17s and Ju 87 Stukas which he immediately attacked. In the ensuing fight Carey destroyed one Do 17 and two of the Stukas. Carey remained in France with 3 Squadron until May 3rd when he was himself shot down by the rear gunner of a Do 17. He was taken to a Belgian hospital for a short time and then returned to England. When he left France, Carey had nine enemy aircraft to his credit.

In late June Carey was pronounced fit for duty and was posted back to 43 Squadron as a flight commander. The unit saw constant action during the Battle of Britain from their base in Southern England and became one of the period's top scoring squadrons. Carey, the leading ace of the unit, had increased his total to eighteen by the end of August, when he was again shot down and wounded. He returned to 43 Squadron in late September at Utsworth, but was shortly transferred to No. 52 Operational Training Unit at Debden as an instructor. After a few months, Carey was posted back to a combat squadron joining 245 Squadron at Ballyhalbert, Northern Ireland.

In January 1942 he was reassigned to

135 Squadron operating from Rangoon and Magwe in Burma. Here again Carey achieved the unit's first victory when in mid-January he destroyed a Japanese fighter. In February, shortly after his promotion to Wing Commander, Carey led his wing on a strafing attack to the Japanese airfield at Moulmein. Upon their arrival over the airfield, the unit was met by a large formation of enemy fighters. A swirling melee filled the skies over the field and during the fighting Carey sent two of the enemy down in flames. Carey accounted for at least ten additional victories while in the Pacific Theater, but due to the loss of all records during the retreat by Allied forces, the true score will never be known.

He returned to England in 1943 and was sent to gunnery school for a refresher course before returning to duty as Fighter Wing Leader in the Air Defense of Calcutta, India. He was then given the task of forming and leading the first Air Fighting Training Unit in India at Armarda Road. Carey remained in this capacity until November 1944 when he was promoted to Group Captain and transferred to the Middle East to command No. 73 Operational Training Unit at Fayid in the Suez Canal Zone. In June 1945 he returned to England as Group Captain (Tactics) at the Central Fighter establishment.

Carey's total victory score has been estimated to be as high as forty while Carey himself places it around thirty. The Royal Air Force officially credits him with twenty-eight. He was decorated with the Distinguished Flying Cross with two bars, the Distinguished Flying Medal, the Air Force Cross, and the American Silver Star. One of the Hurricane Is Carey piloted while with 43 Squadron in 1940 is illustrated on page 42.

DONAHUE, Major Archie
VMF-451
USS Bunker Hill
USMC
(14 Victories)

Archie Donahue was born on October 24, 1917 in Casper, Wyoming and attended local schools until 1934 when he moved to Texas. After completing three years of engineering at the University of Texas, he was accepted as an Aviation Cadet in the Navy and was sent first to Kansas City, Missouri, then to Jacksonville, Florida and finally to Corpus Christi Air Station in Texas. He requested a transfer to the Marine Corps upon graduation and was commissioned as a Second Lieutenant in February 1942. Donahue was posted to Norfolk, Virginia for a short while before being assigned to VMF-112 (Wolf Pack). VMF-112 arrived at Guadalcanal in September 1942 flying Grumman F4F-4 Wildcats and immediately went into action. Between September 1942 and June 1943, Donahue was credited with nine enemy aircraft in the skies over Guadalcanal, achieving the first in his F4F-4 and the remaining eight in the newly acquired F4U-1 Corsair. On May 13, 1943 he destroyed five Mitsubishi A6M3 Zeros in a single engagement, then returned to the United States with VMF-112 in June at which time the unit was disbanded. Serving as Flight Officer at El Toro Air Station in California, Donahue was, in late 1944, assigned to VMF-451 and given the responsibility for making the unit carrier qualified.

On February 16, 1945 VMF-451 began combat operations from the deck of the USS *Bunker Hill* carrying out a fighter sweep over Tokyo and for the next three months Donahue took part in continuous bombing, strafing, and close support missions for the landings at Iwo Jima and Okinawa and in Allied operations against the Japanese mainland. On April 12th, Donahue was again credited with five victories in a single engagement in a dogfight over Okinawa. In May the *Bunker Hill* was attacked and severely damaged during a Kamikaze attack and was forced to retire with her Air Group from active combat. Donahue returned to the States and was put in command of a squadron at El Toro before being posted to Quantico, Virginia where he remained until his release from service. For his actions Donahue was decorated with the Navy Cross, three Distinguished Flying Crosses and five Air Medals. He flew 159 combat missions over Guadalcanal and 56 from the deck of the *Bunker Hill*, and was credited with a total of fourteen confirmed aerial victories. One of the F4U-1s piloted by Donahue from USS *Bunker Hill* in March 1945 is illustrated on page 38.

Henderson Field on Guadalcanal (Cactus) during the summer of 1942, displays its lineup of F4F Wildcats made up of assorted Marine and Navy units.

By early 1943, Donahue was flying the new Vought F4U Corsair, the most versatile fighter in the Pacific. In addition to possessing a 50 mph. speed advantage over the Wildcat, Corsair could also haul a ton of bombs. Shown here . . . two 500 pounders.

The struggle for Guadalcanal and the Solomon chain lasted late into 1943 and field conditions were primitive throughout. Here, using a homemade coconut log hoist, groundcrewmen boresight the guns of an F4U-1.

DONALDSON, Group Captain Arthur H.
263 Squadron
Royal Air Force
(5.5 Victories)

A delight to fly, heavily armed and a very hot fighter, the Westland Whirlwind did not live up to its potential for two reasons: constant troubles with its Rolls Royce Peregrine engine, and the appearance of the de Havilland Mosquito, which could do everything the Whirlwind could, do it better, and was built of non-strategic materials. Armament of four 20mm cannon was very heavy for 1939, when first Whirlwind was to have been delivered, but production problems delayed date until the middle of 1941.

Arthur Hay Donaldson, one of three brothers to fly in the RAF and be awarded the Distinguished Service Order, was born in Weymouth, England on January 9, 1915. Entering the Royal Air Force, he was commissioned as a Acting Pilot Officer on March 16, 1934. His training began at No. 3 Flying Training School, Grantham, Lincolnshire where he remained until March 3, 1935, at which time he was posted to 56 Squadron at North Weald, Essex, flying the Bristol Bulldog. A year later, Donaldson was reassigned to 24 Squadron at Hendon, and in May 1938, he was posted to the Central Flying School at Upavon, Wilts, for Flying Instructors and then sent to No. 1 Flying School, Leuchars, Scotland, for naval pilot training. In January 1939 Donaldson was transferred back to the Central Flying School, and remained here during the Battles of France and Britan, despite five years of intensive and diversified flying experience.

On January 19, 1941, Donaldson was posted to 242 Canadian Fighter Squadron at Martlesham Heath, Suffolk (commanded by the famous legless Douglas Bader). Flying Hawker Hurricanes, he flew his first operational sortie on February 4th on patrol duty to the north coast of France. In February he was reassigned to 263 Squadron armed with the new Westland Whirlwind twin-engine fighter and assumed command of this unit. Donaldson flew with this group for a year being credited with several damaged aircraft and destroying many on the ground during strafing and support sorties, but was yet to gain his first full air victory. On August 21, 1941, now in command of the Whirlwind Wing, he was decorated with the Distinguished Flying Cross for leading the fighters on low level attacks on Luftwaffe airfields in France. On one of these occasions, Donaldson led an attack on Morlaix Airfield and explosive shells from enemy ground defenses hit his aircraft in three places, one puncturing the cockpit and exploding. The shrapnel burst tore his flight helmet open and knocked him unconscious. When he recovered he found himself over the English Channel. Although badly hit and bleeding profusely from his wounds, Donaldson guided his crippled plane back to his base at Cornwall. He remained in the hospital for several weeks before finally returning to duty.

In April 1942 Donaldson was posted to command the Spitfire Wing at Fairwood Common, Wales, and in August was reassigned to command the Spitfire Wing at Takali, Malta. On the 23rd he took part in the first offensive sweep over Sicily. He shared in the destruction of a Do 217 and a Macchi 202 during September, and in early October destroyed a Ju 88 bomber. On the 11th, Donaldson was credited with a Me 109 and another Ju 88, and on the 14th destroyed still another Ju 88.

On October 15th, he was again shot down. Separated from his unit, he had pushed on through a screen of Luftwaffe fighters to set fire to an enemy bomber, when he was jumped by two Me 109s. He lost two fingers of his left hand and suffered both head and foot wounds. For this action Donaldson was awarded the Distinguished Service Order on October 22nd, but bad fortune continued to plague him.

On October 31st, Donaldson was being flown out of Malta as a wounded stretcher case on a B-24 Liberator, when the aircraft crashed into the sea off Gibraltar. Donaldson was one of only three survivors. After additional recuperation, he was posted to command the Ibsley Fighter Station in March 1943.

For his actions as Wing Commander on Malta, Donaldson was decorated with a bar to his Distinguished Flying Cross. This citation ackowledged that at the beginning of 1942 the Luftwaffe bombers carried out their last great blitz against the Island of Malta. In ten days the Luftwaffe lost 131 aircraft for the loss of only 13 Spitfire pilots. Donaldson's own Wing destroyed 51 of these without a single loss. He also led three separate attacks on enemy airfields in Sicily during which his Wing destroyed 10 Luftwaffe aircraft in dogfights and an additional 30 on the ground. The citation ends with: "Throughout, his leadership, careful planning, and personal courage were an inspiration to all."

In December 1943, Donaldson was promoted to Group Captain and posted to command Coltishal Fighter Sector, Norfolk. In March 1945 he was posted as Group Captain Operations No. 11 Fighter Wing in Burma and returned at war's end to command the Lincolnshire Fighter Sector in November.

One of the Westland Whirlwinds flown by Donaldson as Commander of the Whirlwind Wing is illustrated on page 39.

DUKE, Squadron Leader Neville F.
112 Squadron
Royal Air Force
(29 Victories)

Neville Frederick Duke, born on January 11, 1922 at Tonbridge, Kent, was interested in flying at an early age and this can be directly related to watching the aircraft fly over Tonbridge from the RAF bases at Biggin Hill and Kenly. Not only did he build model planes, but he collected photographs of all types and at the age of ten took his first flight. In 1939 he graduated from high school and rather than pursue an advanced education, waited six months until his eighteenth birthday at which time he would be eligible for a pilot's certificate. In January 1940 Duke applied and was accepted for pilot's training.

Duke received his basic flight instruction in Tiger Moths at No. 13 Elementary Flying School in White Walthem, his advanced training in Miles Masters at No. 5 Flying Training School at Sealand and Ternhill, and finally checked out in Supermarine Spitfires at No. 58 Operational Training Unit in Grangemouth, Scotland. After completion of his instruction Duke was posted to 92 Squadron at Biggin Hill on April 1, 1941. His first combat consisted of flying fighter sweeps and patrol duty over Northern France, but he did not score until June 25th when he was credited with a Me 109 over Dunkirk. He was returning from an escort mission over St. Omer, France when he sighted the Me 109 attacking another Spitfire. Duke immediately jumped the Luftwaffe fighter and opened fire. He watched as the Me 109 belched smoke and headed toward the beaches below. Duke's next combat assignment saw him flying wingman for another great RAF ace, Adolph "Sailor" Malan, from whom he learned almost all there was to learn about combat fighter tactics. He scored one more victory with 92 Squadron, a Me 109 over France, before he was posted to 112 Squadron in the Western Desert in November.

It was November 12th when Duke reported to 112 Squadron at Sidi Hannish, and received his introduction to the Curtiss P-40 Tomahawk. It took him less than a week to master the American built fighter and destroy his first enemy fighter in the desert. It was not too long after that Duke himself became someone else's victory as he was shot down on November 30th. After crash landing, he set out on foot for friendly lines and was picked up in a short time by a British Army truck and returned to 112 Squadron. On December 4th he added a Macchi 200 to his score but the following day was again forced to crashland his Tomahawk. He remained off of flying status for two weeks before returning to duty, but quickly let the Luftwaffe and *Regia Aeronautica* know he was back when he was credited with a Me 109 before Christmas.

With the beginning of 1942, 112 Squadron was sent to Suez to re-equip with the Kittyhawk, an improved version of the P-40, and then moved back to their base at Msus. Offensive operations against the Axis were somewhat limited over the next few months as 112 Squadron was ordered to support the British retreat to El Alamein and their sorties were composed primarily of bombing and strafing against Rommel's advancing forces. Nevertheless, Duke was able to destroy his eighth enemy aircraft during one of these sorties. It was during this time that Duke praised the P-40's ability to absorb punishment, even though he had been rather disappointed with it when he switched over from Spitfires.

"I must tell you that my initial impressions of the Curtiss were not good after Spit Vs at Biggin Hill. But after flying it, I came to modify my views. If the P-40 had a fault, it was over-built. In other words, it was too good in unnecessary areas, but its solid frame and construction allowed it to withstand terrific amounts of battle damage, even if this same construction made it too heavy. As a result, climb was very poor. It was not as agile as the 109 or the Spitfire. However, that same great weight allowed it to accelerate very well in a dive. It was easy to fly, maneuverable, carried enormous amounts of ammunition and had better range than any other fighter in the Western Desert. As a gun platform, it was unequalled, and although the Kittyhawk replaced the earlier Tomahawk's two .50 caliber cowl guns and four wing mounted .30s, with six .50 caliber wing guns, I preferred to fly with only four wing guns to save weight and improve performance. The Curtiss' greatest asset was its ruggedness. On one occasion I lost one elevator, an aileron, my flaps and was full of holes. The lowest speed at which I could control the Tomahawk in that condition was 150 mph. I crashlanded it at Tobruk and walked away without a scratch. Another time a 109's cannon shell exploded in my wing while I was in a very tight turn at low altitude. The impact flipped the aircraft over on its back and when I recovered, we hit the ground at very high speed, smashing the aircraft flat on the desert floor. Again I walked away."

In March, Duke was reassigned to the Fighter School at El Ballah, Egypt as an instructor. He remained at the school instructing young pilots in the tactics of combat flying with the Tomahawk and Kittyhawk until November when he was posted back to 92 Squadron, now at Sidi Barrani. Less than a week after Duke's arrival, the unit moved to Msus to begin fighter sweeps against El Agheila and Agedabia in support of the now advancing Allies. The offensive moved quickly, and 92 Squadron moved with it. With all the activity there was little chance for aerial engagements, but with the new year of 1943 the squadron settled at Tamet and once again started

Mainstay of the RAF in the Western Desert was the Curtiss Tomahawk. Originally transferred to the British from unfilled French order, the export version of the Curtiss P-40 or Hawk 81-A, had only a pair of .50 caliber guns mounted in the cowling. The improved Tomahawk IIA added two wing guns, additional armor plate and self sealing fuel tanks. Still another improvement, the Tomahawk IIB, shown here, added another pair of wing guns, for a total of six .50 caliber weapons. Known to the U.S. Air Corps as the P-40C, 930 of these aircraft went to the RAF. Duke flew both the IIA and IIB.

to find the Luftwaffe willing to fight in the skies over the desert. Duke destroyed a Macchi 202 on January 8th and was credited with two more on January 11th. Again, on January 21st Duke accounted for two more enemy aircraft and received the news he had been awarded a bar to his Distinguished Flying Cross.

In March Duke was made Acting Squadron Leader of 92 Squadron at Medanine and experienced a very eventful week in which he shot down seven enemy planes. On March 1st he destroyed two Macchi 202s on one mission and two days later, he destroyed a Me 109. On March 4th Duke accounted for a pair of Me 109s and on March 7th sent another two to the desert floor in flames on separate sorties. In mid-March, 92 Squadron moved up to Bu Ghara in their continuing attempt to maintain a forward base as close as possible to retreating Axis air units. From here, on March 29th, Duke achieved his twentieth victory by destroying a Me 109 while on patrol duty near Gabes. He accounted for two more victories before being posted to an Operational Training Unit at Abu Sueir, Egypt as Chief Flying Instructor.

Duke remained in this capacity until February 1944, at which time he was posted back to operation duty with 145 Squadron in Italy as Squadron Leader. After numerous uneventful patrols over Anzio and Cassino, the squadron finally met the Luftwaffe over Northern Italy. Duke added four more Luftwaffe fighters to his score before he again was shot down on June 7th. The good luck he enjoyed in the desert had not left him, however, and after a few hours he was located and picked up by Allied troops. Moving to Loreto, Italy, for the conflict above the Gothic Line, Duke achieved his final two victories on September 3rd near Rimini when he flamed a pair of Me 109s.

Duke ended the war as one of the top RAF and Allied aces with twenty-nine enemy aircraft destroyed and was decorated with the Distinguished Service Order, the Distinguished Flying Cross and two bars, the Order of the British Empire, and the Air Force Cross. One of the Curtiss P-40s piloted by Duke with 112 Squadron in the Western desert is illustrated on page 35.

FLEMING, Lt. Francis M.
United States Navy
VF-16
USS Lexington
USN
(7.5 Victories)

Born in Cathlamet, Washington on October 4, 1916, Frank Fleming enlisted in the U.S. Navy in October 1941 after completing two years at the University of Portland. Having already gained a private pilot's license in 1940, Fleming was assigned to preliminary flight training at NAS Sandpoint, Seattle and then to Pensacola, Florida. He completed his training for carrier duty at Opa Locka, Florida (near Miami) received his wings in September of 1942, and was assigned to Air Group 16 aboard the new *USS Lexington,* leaving with the carrier from the Boston Navy Yard in 1943. Fleming's first aerial combat came on November 23, 1943. He was part of a routine 12 plane Combat Air Patrol and was vectored out to intercept 24 Zeros. With the altitude advantage and surprise on his side, Fleming was credited with destroying 2½ enemy aircraft in his first encounter, the 12 Hellcats destroying 20 of the 24 Zeros.

On November 24 he again found himself on Combat Air Patrol in the same area and was vectored to intercept numerous bogeys at 23,000 feet. Sighting of the enemy force disclosed 24 Zeros and 2 Bettys. In the ensuing melee Fleming was credited with 2 more Zeros, raising his total to 4½ in two days.

His next victory, which raised Fleming to Ace status, was recorded while supporting the Army landings in Hollandia, New Guinea where he destroyed a twin-engine "Sally" in April 1944.

On June 19, 1944 Fleming was part of a flight of seven Grumman Hellcats assigned to strafing and rocket runs over Guam. After destroying several planes on the ground, the group was recalled to provide low level protection to the Fleet, as there had been reports of numerous formations of Japanese aircraft approaching at all altitudes. This was the start of the "Marianas Turkey Shoot" in which over 400 Japanese planes were shot down and destroyed in a single day. Fleming's roommate, Ralph Hanks, was leading the division of seven Hellcats, and Fleming was flying Section Lead in the 2nd flight of four, which had been reduced to three when one of the planes (Fleming's wingman) had developed engine trouble. When they arrived at the Fleet, it was under heavy attack and the ships were firing a continuous barrage of 5 inch anti-aircraft fire from the vertical to the horizontal. Flying at 3000 feet, well out of range of the Fleet's ack-ack, Fleming suddenly spotted other planes at 2 o'clock and 180° to his position. Unable to identify them, he pulled off to follow and for reasons unexplained failed to radio an alert to the remainder of his Section. Committing the cardinal sin of a fighter pilot, Fleming went off alone and overtook the aircraft from the right rear quarter; identifying them as Nakajima B6N Jills, Japanese torpedo bombers, positioning themselves for a run on the Fleet. Fleming managed to pull in directly behind the enemy aircraft and began firing. The first plane caught fire and burned violently, crashing into the Pacific. Fleming repeated this maneuver and the second aircraft went into the water from 100 feet. Concentrating on getting the third plane, Fleming finally looked into his

Lt. Fleming poses with some personal missives intended for delivery to Japanese Battleship *Nagato*, prior to launch from *Randolph*.

rear view mirror and noticed a Zero closing fast from above and astern, in perfect position for the kill.

The Zero opened fire, but missed badly, giving Fleming time to turn toward the Fleet and into the friendly barrage. Too low to dive, and unable to outrun the Zero at low altitudes, Fleming had selected the only avenue of escape open to him. The Zero turned away as the two planes approached the ack-ack, and Fleming, his Hellcat scarred with a number of shrapnel holes from the Fleet's fire, gave chase. The Zero immediately slowed down hoping to get in behind Fleming, who used everything from flaps to landing gear to stay behind his enemy. The Zero then dove directly down, leveling out just over the water's surface. Fleming nosed down, firing short bursts, lifting his nose again to prevent crashing into the sea. Pieces flew off the Zero, it smoked, it shuddered, but it would not go down.

Fleming's outboard guns ran out of ammunition, due to the strafing runs conducted earlier in the day. When his mid-guns quit, Fleming broke off the encounter and returned to the *Lexington*. He was credited with 2 aircraft destroyed and 1 probable, the Zero, to raise his total score to 7½. For his actions on this day, he was decorated with the Silver Star.

A few weeks later, VF-16 returned to the United States for leave and reorganization. Six months later, Fleming and VF-16 were aboard the new carrier *USS BonHomme Richard* and headed for combat in the Western Pacific.

Air Group 16 was removed from *Bon Homme Richard* in Hawaii to make way for another Air Group from the old *Enterprise* which had been damaged by *Kamikazes* and was on its way to Bremerton for repair. VF-16 was finally put aboard a "Jeep" carrier and taken to San Pedro Bay in the Philippines where they were assigned to *USS Randolph*. By early July, Fleming was flying support, escort, and strike missions against the coast of Japan from Kiyushu Island in the North to Hokkaida Island in the south. He flew his last strike on the morning of August 8, 1945, the day word was released that Japan had surrendered. He remained with the *Randolph* and flew patrol duty until the treaty was signed and troops put ashore from the Fleet.

Involved in every action against every island group of consequence except the Solomons, Bougainville, Rabaul, Iwo Jima, Philippines, Formosa, and Okinawa, Fleming logged over 500 hours of combat time and flew over 100 missions on two combat tours. He was decorated with the Silver Star, two Distinguished Flying Crosses, five Air Medals, two Presidential Unit Citations, the Pacific Theater and seven Battle Stars (denoting major battles), and numerous other Campaign Ribbons.

The F6F-3 Grumman Hellcat flown by Fleming from *USS Lexington* in late 1943 is illustrated on page 36.

Not the fighter the F4U Corsair was, Grumman's F6F Hellcat was equipped with the same basic powerplant (Pratt & Whitney R-2800, eighteen cylinder radial) and was a much easier aircraft to fly, particularly by new, inexperienced pilots fresh out of flying school. Here, Hellcats take off from USS *Randolph* for end of war strikes on Japan.

GABRESKI, Lt. Colonel Francis S.
United States Army Air Force
61st Fighter Sqdn.
8th Air Force
(28 Victories)

Francis S. "Gabby" Gabreski, born on January 28, 1919 in Oil City, Pennsylvania, attended elementary and high school in his home town, graduating in June 1938. He then enrolled at Notre Dame University in South Bend, Indiana for Pre-Medical study, leaving school in July 1940 to enter pilot training with the United States Army at Parks Air College, Maxwell Air Force Base, Alabama. Completing his basic pilot's instruction, Gabreski was then assigned to the Southeast Air Training Center, graduating in March 1941. He was then posted to the 45th Fighter Squadron, 15th Fighter Group at Wheeler Field, Hawaii where he remained until October 1942. (Although at Wheeler Field during the attack on Pearl Harbor, he did not engage in any aerial combat with the Japanese.) He was then transferred to the European Theatre of Operations as a member of the 8th Air Force Fighter Command, serving as a Liaison Officer to the Polish Air Force contingent. Gabreski flew over twenty combat missions with the Polish Wing in Supermarine Spitfire Vs, but did not score.

In February 1943, Gabreski was assigned to the 61st Fighter Squadron, 56th Fighter Group as a flight leader. He took command of the Squadron in June and was promoted to the rank of Major on July 19, 1943. Gabreski had yet to destroy his first enemy aircraft, but, finally, on August 24th he was credited with destroying a Fw 190. His score continued to rise as the 56th flew increased bomber support and strafing sorties inside German occupied territory. On November 26th, he reached ace status when he downed a pair of Luftwaffe Me 110s near Oldenburg, Germany.

In early January, 1944, Gabreski was made Deputy Operations Officer for the 56th, but resumed command of the 61st in April. He was credited with his final victory on July 5, 1944 when he destroyed a Me 109G. On July 20th, while leading his unit returning from an escort mission, Gabreski crashlanded after a strafing run on the Bassinheim Airfield. Unhurt, he was taken prisoner and sent to Stalag Luft 1 where he remained until his liberation in April 1945.

Gabreski ended the war as the third highest scoring United States combat pilot and compiled over 166 combat missions and over 500 combat hours piloting Spitfires and P-47 Thunderbolts. He was decorated with the Distinguished Flying Cross, the Distinguished Service Cross, the Silver Star with Oak Leaf Cluster, the Legion of Merit, the Bronze Star, the Air Medal, and many foreign awards including the Polish Cross of Valor, the Belgium Croix de Guerre, and the British Distinguished Flying Cross. His 28 victories were recorded in only 11 months.

Lt. Col. Francis Gabreski's red-nosed bubble-topped P-47D. Auxiliary belly tank carried 110 gallons, extending combat loaded range to 925 miles.

GALLAND, General Adolf
JG 26
Luftwaffe
(104 Victories)

Adolf Galland was born in Westerholt in March of 1912. After graduation from school in Westphalia, he started flying gliders and by the time he was twenty-two had completed pilot training with *Lufthansa*, the German national airline. In late 1934 Galland joined the Luftwaffe and was posted to his first unit, JG 2 "Richthofen", in 1935. He began flying combat as a member of the famed Condor Legion in the Spanish Civil War two years later, and it was here that he conceived the fighter tactics that he would later use against the Allied powers. Galland commanded 3/J.88 until his tour of duty in Spain ended on May 24, 1938. In 1939 he was assigned to JG 27 as Operations Officer, and with the outbreak of WW II, scored his first victories on May 12, 1940 near Liege, Belgium, when he was credited with downing three Hurricanes. In June, Galland was transferred and given command of III/JG 26.

As *Gruppenkommandeur* of III/JG 26, Galland was credited with two victories on his first day of command, and in July was promoted to the rank of Major which he held during the Battle of Britain. Between July and September, Galland increased his score to forty at the expense of the RAF and was decorated with the Knights Cross on August 1st. On November 1st he was promoted to the rank of Lt. Colonel and given full command of JG 26.

On June 21, 1941, Galland was himself shot down for the first time when, after he had flamed a RAF Spitfire he made the basic error of paying more attention to his fallen victim than to his own vulnerability. Attacked from behind by pursuing Spitfires, he was badly wounded and his Me 109 set aflame. Galland managed to bail out and was picked up by German ground forces. He spent some time in the hospital before returning to duty with JG 26. For his actions, Galland was decorated with the newly designated award of the Swords to add to his Oak Leaves, the first German pilot to be decorated with this honor.

By December of 1941, Galland had fought through the Battles of France and Britain (at the end of which his score had risen to fifty-seven confirmed victories), and had been appointed General of the Fighter Arm after the death of his friend, Werner Mölders. At age 29 Galland was the youngest General in any of Germany's armed forces.

After his promotion to General of the Fighter Arm, Galland was given responsibility for escorting the German battleships *Gneisenau* and *Scharnhorst* from Brest to Kiel. This operation was primarily dependent upon the support of continuous Luftwaffe fighter cover for the ships during their dash. Without the fighter cover the ships would certainly fall victim to the RAF. Under Galland's leadership the operation was hailed in Germany as a fantastic feat of strategy, and Galland was acclaimed a tactical genius for his efforts. Despite the accolades he was not happy with his new found success and wanted to return to combat flying.

His requests for combat were refused and he remained in staff positions until January 1945, when he was finally granted return to active combat duty as commander of the newly formed JG 44. This jet unit, composed of highly skilled Luftwaffe pilots and many of its highest scoring aces, was to become known as the "Squadron of Experts". Galland led them until April 26, 1945 when he was again wounded and ended his fighting with enemy shrapnel in his leg. After a short recuperation in a German hospital, he was taken prisoner and finally released in 1947.

One of the "first to last" pilots of World War II, Galland survived the conflict with 104 confirmed victories, all against the Western Allies. He was also decorated with the Knights Cross with Diamonds. Had it not been for his service as a staff officer for three years, his total victories would have surely been higher. Galland was considered by most of the Luftwaffe's pilots as that service's finest military mind and was highly respected by both his subordinates and superiors.

Two of Galland's aircraft are illustrated on page 41.

GENTILE, Captain Donald S.
336th Fighter Squadron
4th Fighter Group
8th Air Force
(21.83 Victories)

Donald Salvatore Gentile was born on December 6, 1920 in Piqua, Ohio and learned to fly before he was graduated from high school. He enlisted in the Royal Air Force after he had tried, and failed, to join the United States Army Air Forces, being unable to pass depth perception tests. He was sent to Canada where he received his flight training before being shipped to England and posted to 133 "Eagle" Squadron with other American volunteers. He was promoted to Flight Officer in December 1941, and flew his first operational mission on June 22, 1942. On August 19th, Gentile was credited with his first two victories when he destroyed a Ju 88 and a Fw 190 while on escort duty with RAF Bomber Command over Dieppe, France.

On September 16, 1942 he was transferred from the RAF to the 8th Air Force as the 336th Fighter Squadron was formed from 133 Squadron. He continued to fly the British Spitfire as a section leader on operational missions over Europe until December 31, 1942 when he effected the transition to the P-47 Thunderbolt. He scored his first victories in this new fighter on January 5, 1944 when he destroyed a Fw 190 in the skies over Holland. Nine days later, Gentile scored again, downing two more Fw 190s, and on February 25th destroyed his fifth Fw 190 while on cover duty over Germany, thus making him an ace.

On March 3rd, Gentile and his wingman took off under adverse weather conditions and set course for Hamburg, Germany, where they were to assist in the escort of heavy bombers that were to bomb enemy installations in that city. After approximately an hour of flying, they sighted a formation of fifty Luftwaffe Do. 217s with a cover of over 200 Focke-Wulfe 190s. Knowing the formation was on its way to attack and break up the American formation, Gentile dived in to attack. During the ensuing engagement, he destroyed two Fw 190s and damaged one Do. 217. It was later learned by Allied intelligence that one of the Fw 190s destroyed by Gentile had been piloted by Kurt von Meyer, a Luftwaffe ace with over 150 victories.

Five days later, on March 8th, Gentile again distinguished himself by attacking a large force of enemy Me 109s, with only his wingman as support, succeeded in downing four of them. Upon breaking up the Luftwaffe threat, Gentile picked up a straggling Allied bomber and escorted it back to friendly territory.

Between March 9th and April 7th, Gentile, now flying the P-51 Mustang, increased his score to nineteen. On March 18th he destroyed a Fw 190, on the 23rd he was credited with two Me 109s. On the 29th he downed another Me 109 and two more Fw 190s, and on April 1st destroyed still another Me 109.

On April 8, 1944, Gentile, now a Captain, again displayed skill and courage as a fighter pilot by leading the 336th Fighter Squadron in an attack against approximately fifty Luftwaffe fighters that were attacking a formation of American Liberator bombers. In the dogfight over Brunswick, Gentile was separated from his Squadron and was set upon by three enemy fighters. Despite the fact he was outnumbered, Gentile successfully evaded the enemy fire and managed to destroy all three of his opponents.

In May 1944, Gentile returned to the United States to participate in a War Bond tour. He attended the Dayton AAF Vandalia Flight Section School Branch and was graduated on December 21, 1944 in Airplane Performance Flight Test and Instrumentation Course, all weather Flying Course, and Blind Flying and Landing Course. He was then assigned to Wright Field as a test pilot and finished the war in this position.

In the course of his combat career, Captain Gentile established one of the most outstanding records ever to be recorded by an American pilot. He flew over 185 combat missions for a total of 387 hours. He was officially credited with destroying thirty-two enemy aircraft (21.83 in the air), nine probables and six damaged. He achieved this record during a period when the vaunted Luftwaffe was at its peak and possessed numerically superior aircraft manned by fearless and determined pilots. Gentile's courage and resourcefulness speaks for itself in the number of enemy aircraft to his credit. His fellow pilots say of him that he was always the first to sight the enemy and always the first to break away and engage in battle regardless of the odds. He was respected by his fellow pilots as well as his superior officers for his professional skill and his fighting spirit.

Gentile was decorated with many awards including the Distinguished Service Cross with one Oak Leaf Cluster, the Distinguished Flying Cross with one Silver Oak Leaf Cluster and two Bronze Oak Leaf Clusters, the Air Medal with three Oak Leaf Clusters, the World War II Victory Medal, the British Star, the *Croce al Merito de Guerra* (Italy), and the Croix de Guerre with Palm (Belgium).

Goring, Luftwaffe Commander in Chief, once said of Gentile and his wingman, John Godfrey, that he would gladly sacrifice two full Luftwaffe Squadrons for the capture or death of this team. Ironically, Gentile was killed after the war in a plane crash.

Major Hans "Assi" Hahn, already holder of Knights Cross, poses with mascot which provided him with nickhame.

HAHN, Major Hans "Assi"
JG 2
Luftwaffe
(108 Victories)

Born on April 4, 1914 in Gotha/Thüringen, Hans "Assi" Hahn graduated from high school during Easter week 1934, and immediately joined the German Army as part of the 14th Infantry Regiment. As a lieutenant, he transferred to the newly authorized Luftwaffe in 1935, receiving his pilots training at Celle on the Lüneburger Heath, and just after the 1936 Olympiade was assigned to ZG 26, "Horst Wessel", at Werl in Westphalia. His commander was Major Theo Osterkamp, an ace of the First World War. In 1937, the Fighter School at Werneuchen, near Berlin, was formed and Osterkamp was made Commanding Officer with Hahn assigned to instructor duty.

Although an experienced pilot Hahn did not go to Spain and, in 1938, he was transferred to Zerbst as a member of JG 3. During the invasion of Poland in 1939, he served with a home defense unit protecting the central German war industry from aerial attacks, which never materialized.

In the winter of 1939, Hahn became a member of newly formed II/JG 2, "Richthofen", and commander of the 4th Staffel. Until the start of the Battle of France, his unit was responsible for the protection of Bremerhaven and its nearby island chain, Hahn entering actual combat for the first time on May 10, 1940 during the campaigns against Holland, Belgium and France. On May 14th he accounted for his first victories when he destroyed two Spitfires over the Maas River near Brussels. His aircraft was an Me 109 E.

Still flying the 109E, Hahn and II/JG 2 were then posted to the Channel Coast for the remainder of the Battle of France and the Battle of Britain, all his combat flying being directed against the RAF. His score continued to mount and on September 23, 1940 over London, Hahn was credited with his twentieth victory. The following day he was decorated with the Knights Cross.

Hahn assumed command of II/JG 2 in the early winter of 1940 and by the summer of 1941 had more than doubled his score to forty-two confirmed victories. Still flying from the Channel Coast and transitioning between the Me 109F and the newer Fw 190, Hahn engaged RAF fighters over Brest, Cherbourg, and Le Havre. He was awarded the Oak Leaves in early fall and became only the thirty-second German serviceman to achieve this level.

Promoted to Major on December 31, 1942, Hahn continued in command of II/JG 2 until November 1942 when he was transferred to the Northern Russian Front to take command of II/JG 54. At this time Hahn's victory total stood at sixty-eight, and he now left the Fw 190.

Once again back in the cockpit of an Me 109, Major Hahn was assigned responsibility for the northern sector, or zone, from the Ilmen Sea to Leningrad. His score continued to increase, and on January 26, 1943 he destroyed his 100th enemy aircraft. Raising his total to 108 by February 20th, Hahn although not knowing it, had downed his final plane of the war. On February 21st while on a ground support and strafing mission over Russian territory, Hahn's aircraft was damaged by infantry and anti-aircraft fire and he was forced to crash land near Waldei. He was immediately taken prisoner by Russian forces and remained in confinement as a prisoner of war until his release in 1950.

Two of the aircraft flown by Hahn during the war are illustrated (pg. 56). The first is the Me 109F he piloted as *Kommandeur* of II/JG 2 in the early summer of 1941 just prior to the unit's re-equipping with Fw 190s. The second aircraft is the one in which Hahn achieved his final victories and the one in which he crash landed behind Russian lines. This plane, a Me 109G, was repaired by Russian Forces and sent to Moscow in mid-1943 to be displayed as a war trophy. It remained there until war's end.

HERGET, Major Wilhelm
ZG 76
Luftwaffe
(72 victories)

The diminutive, 35 year old Herget (right) with his crew: Staff Sgt. Emil Gross (center) and Sgt. Hans Liebherr, astride their Me 110G coded M8-HP. Note additional bracket for armored front windshield.

Born in Stuttgart, Germany on June 30, 1910, Hergert, a printer by trade, received instructions in flying at his own expense, in 1935. That October he joined the Luftwaffe and was sent to Boeblingen for further flight training. For the next two years he served as a sergeant before being posted to Wuerburg with Fighter Reconnaissance unit F 123. In May 1937 he was transferred to Schleissheim near Munich for advanced fighter training, after which he was promoted to Lieutenant and assigned to JG 234 at Mannheim/Sandhofen. He saw his first combat with this unit in 1938, when he took part in action over the Sudetenland, against Czech Avias, flying Me 109Bs from Bad Aibling. On August 25, 1939 Herget was transferred to II ZG 76 (Destroyer Wing) at Gablingen/Augsburg.

He flew with ZG 76 during the invasions of Belgium and France, and was credited with his first victory on May 25, 1940 when he destroyed a Royal Air Force Hurricane over Dunkirk, while piloting a Me 110C. Four days later he destroyed a Spitfire in the same area. On June 6th he shot down a French Curtiss P-36 near Cherbourg for his third victory and then retired with his unit for a short time to prepare for the Battle of Britain.

From August 10th until the end of September, 1940 Herget took part in 20 raids on the London area and accounted for 9 more RAF planes (three Hurricanes and six Spitfires) all of them shot down over the Greater London area.

From October 1940 until April 1941, Herget continued to fly with ZG 76 between Amsterdam, Holland and Trondheim, Norway escorting Germany Navy convoys. In April he was sent with one staffel of ZG 76 to Iraq to fly Me 110Ds with insurgent forces against the British. In this action, the unit's aircraft bore the markings of the Iraqi Air Force, but retained the shark's teeth made famous by ZG 76. Herget made over 20 attacks on British troops near Bagdad, before returning to Germany in June, once again assuming the role of convoy escort until the end of 1941.

In January 1942, Herget began his nightfighting career in "Raum" (area or zone) 6 with NJG 1 near St. Trond, Belgium. In April he was transferred to "Raum" 7 and operated from airfields at Juvincourt and Laon/Athis, France with NJG 3. It was here, on April 6th, that Herget accounted for his first night victory, a Handley-Page Hampden. On October 1, 1942, he was transferred to I/NJG 4 as Commander flying from Florennes, Belgium.

For the next 18 months his unit moved about from Florennes to Mons, Cambrai, La Rouchele and Bouillon. In August 1944, shortly after the Allied invasion of France, the unit left Belgium and returned to Germany where they were based at the Rhein/Main airfield in Frankfurt and nearby auxiliary fields, the *gruppe* being split with each *staffel* based at a different location, due to the continued Allied bombing of the airfields.

On January 1, 1945 Herget was transferred to JV 44, the Me 262 unit under General Adolf Galland, and achieved his final victory with this unit on April 27, 1945 when he destroyed an American P-47 Thunderbolt near Bad Aibling. One week later, on May 2nd, Herget, himself, was shot down while flying reconnaissance in a Fieseler *Storch* and was taken prisoner by American troops and sent to England where he stayed until the cessation of hostilities. Herget ended the war with 72 confirmed victories, 57 of them as a nightfighter, all but one achieved while flying models of the Me 110. He was decorated with the Knights Cross and Oak Leaves. Of his 57 night victories, all were bombers, 26 were British Lancasters, and eight (three Halifax, and five Lancasters) all fell before his guns on the night of December 20, 1943, an almost phenomenal performance.

Herget's Me 110 is
illustrated on page 60.

HOLLOWELL, Major George L.
VMF-111
USMC
(8 Victories)

George L. Hollowell was born in Kansas City, Kansas on December 6, 1920. He attended Central Grade School and Wyandotte High School in his home town before entering Colorado State University, and later transferring to Kansas State. He enlisted in the United States Naval Reserve on May 3, 1941 as a Seaman Second Class, but was given an honorable discharge on August 6th in order to accept an appointment as an Aviation Cadet. Hollowell completed his flight training at Corpus Christi, Texas and on May 25, 1942 asked to be discharged to accept an appointment as an aviator with the rank of second lieutenant in the United States Marine Corps. His first assignment was with VMF-224, and he was shipped overseas, to Ewa, Oahu, Hawaii.

Hollowell's next stop was the island of Guadalcanal from which VMF-224 operated between August and October. Here, he took part not only in the battles for Guadalcanal, but those of Savo Island and Tulagi. Flying from Henderson Field against the attacking Japanese forces, Hollowell's unit, under the command of Robert Galer, was credited with destroying approximately 50 enemy planes between August and September.

After returning from leave in early 1943, and having been promoted to the rank of Captain, Hollowell remained with VMF-224 for a short period of time before reassignment to VMF-111 "Devil Dogs". He began island hopping in support of the Allied assaults and was based at Samoa, Nanomea, Funifati, Tarawa, Makin, and Kwajalein over the next months, taking part in the first strikes against Mille, Wotje, Jaluit, and Kwajalein. He ended the war with eight confirmed victories, achieved in the skies over Guadalcanal and was decorated with six Distinguished Flying Crosses, one Legion of Merit and twelve Air Medals.

One of the F4U Corsair's flown by Hollowell while attached to VMF-111 is illustrated on page 57

Birdcage F4U-1 Corsair, so named because of the multi-ribbed canopy, was Hollowell's first combat mount during the battle for Guadalcanal. In addition to a near 50 mph. speed advantage over the Japanese Zero, Corsair got full aileron deflection and quick turns at high speeds, a quality the Zero did not have.

JOHNSON, Wing Commander James E.
144 Wing
Royal Air Force
(38 Victories)

James Edgar Johnson was born in Barrow-on-Soar, Leicestershire, England, March 9, 1915 and was educated at local schools prior to entering the University College at Nottingham. He tried to enlist in the Auxiliary Air Force in 1937, but was rejected. In May 1939 Johnson joined the Royal Air Force Voluntary Reserve, a weekend organization similar to England's Territorial Army, and when war broke out on September 3, 1939, was immediately called into active service and posted to pilots' training. After flying in Tiger Moths and Miles Masters, he was sent to Hawarden to transition into the Supermarine Spitfire. From here Johnson was assigned, in August 1940, as a Pilot Officer to 19 Squadron at Duxford, but because of his limited experience in the Spitfire under combat conditions was transferred to 616 Squadron in late 1940 and flew on operational sorties under the leadership of many aces from the Battle of Britain.

Flying as part of the Tangmere Wing, Johnson was fortunate enough to fly with Douglas Bader, the "Legless Wonder", and on June 26th achieved his first victory when he destroyed a Me 109. Johnson soon became wingman for Bader, but flying protective cover for Bader did not offer much opportunity to increase his score. However, on August 9, Bader was shot down and taken prisoner. Johnson evened the score a few minutes later when he sent one of the Luftwaffe attackers down in flames. By September 1941, Johnson had reached "ace status" and with the award of the Distinguished Flying Cross was promoted to flight commander.

Johnson remained with 616 Squadron until July 1942 when he was posted to 610 Squadron as its leader. He led the unit on the Dieppe Raid on August 9th and during the air battles over the flaming beaches, scored a victory against a Fw 190 from the Luftwaffe's JG 2. He remained with 610 Squadron, leading the unit on sweep and interceptor sorties until March 1943, but did not increase his score. In March he was posted to 127 Wing based at Kenley and a few days later, April 3rd, led the Wing on a fighter sweep inside France. The Wing encountered a formation of Fw 190s intent on stopping the Canadian unit and Johnson ordered the attack. He picked out a straggler which had dropped somewhat behind the enemy's main body and closed to within a little over a hundred yards before opening fire. Johnson watched the enemy fighter burst into flames and spin into the landscape around St. Omer. For the remainder of the month, the unit met little opposition from the Luftwaffe during sweep and escort missions, but in May 1943, the German fighters again rose in strength to meet the Allied threat. Within the next two weeks Johnson doubled his total. On June 15th Johnson led his Canadian unit on another fighter sweep into France and over Rouen sighted a formation of approximately a dozen Fw 190s below his two squadrons. Assigning one squadron to top cover he led the second squadron in a diving attack on the enemy fighters. As the Luftwaffe pilots became aware of the impending danger they proceeded to break off in random fashion to evade the attackers, but this proved to be a fruitless effort as the Canadians ripped into them. Johnson picked out one of the Fw 190s and quickly disposed of it with a short burst of cannon fire. A week later Johnson scored again, his fifteenth, when he combined with Canadian ace Robert "Buck" McNair to destroy two Fw 190s near Le Havre.

Between July 19th and July 30th, 127 Wing was detailed to escort several Allied bombing missions to the Luftwaffe airfield at Schipol. During these raids Johnson increased his score to eighteen by destroying a pair of Me 109s. Through the next month and a half, Johnson continued to demonstrate his skill and by the middle of September had a total victory tally of twenty-five, nineteen of which had been destroyed during his five month tour with 127 Wing.

After a six month posting to Fighter Command Headquarters, Johnson returned to combat duty in March 1944

Spit IX built at Castle Bromwich and flown by South African Sqdn., destroyed two aircraft during war. It is one of several which has been restored to flying condition. (Stuart Howe)

in command of 144 Canadian Wing. On April 25th while leading his new unit on a fighter sweep, a flight of six Fw 190s were sighted just ahead of the two Canadian squadrons. Ordering a pursuit, Johnson pulled his aircraft into striking distance after a twenty-mile chase and all six enemy aircraft were shot down. Johnson was credited with two of them, his twenty-sixth and twenty-seventh. Ten days later, he became the highest scoring RAF ace on active operations when he was credited with his twenty-eighth near Lille, France.

On June 15th the Wing moved to a base inside France and the next day Johnson destroyed an intruding Fw 190 just over the airfield. On June 30th he became the RAF's leading ace when he shot down a Me 109 during a fighter sweep sortie (this was based on recorded victories and does not include those of Pattle, whose 40+ victories are in part based on verbal reports). On July 5th, Johnson, again leading the unit on operations, engaged a dozen Me 109s near Alencon. During this action the Wing was credited with the destruction of seven of the enemy and Johnson accounted for two of these to raise his total to thirty-five.

Johnson scored his final victory on September 27th, while on a patrol in the Venlo, Holland area. In the encounter with nine Me 109s, Johnson's own Spitfire was hit and he was forced to break off combat with the enemy. This was to be the first and last time that an aircraft flown by Johnson had been hit by enemy fire. He continued to fly on Operations and ended the war in command of 125 Wing, but failed to add to his victory total. Flying over 1000 combat missions, the majority of which were in command of Canadian Fighter Wings, he was decorated with the Distinguished Service Order with two bars, the Distinguished Flying Cross with bar, and several foreign awards.

Spitfire Mk. IX first reached operational squadrons in July, 1942. Top speed: 404 mph. Range, internal fuel at 220 mph.:434 miles. Armament: Two 20mm cannon, two .50 caliber machine guns, one 500 lb. bomb, two 250 lb. bombs. If bombs deleted, external fuel tank of 190 gallons gave range of 980 miles.

KATO, Colonel Tateo
64TH Sentai
Imperial Japanese Air Force
(18 +Victories)

Tateo Kato, one of the most famous of all Japanese World War II combat pilots, was born on September 28, 1903 in Hokkaido, Japan. The son of a Japanese Army officer, who was killed in action in Manchuria in 1905, Tateo entered the Sendai Army Military Preparatory School on September 1, 1918 from which he graduated in March 1921. Kato was then appointed to the Army Military Academy and two years later he completed his preparatory courses and was assigned to the 25th Infantry Regiment as an Officer Candidate.

Kato returned to the Army Military Academy for advanced training and in 1925, graduated with honors as an officer candidate. In October he was commissioned as a second lieutenant and was assigned to the 6th Air Force Regiment stationed in North Korea.

Kato remained in North Korea until June, 1926, when he returned to Japan and entered the Tokorozawa Army Air Force Flying School. He graduated from flying school at the top of his class exactly one year later and was returned to North Korea to rejoin the 6th Air Force Regiment.

For nearly 10 years Kato, now a captain, remained an instructor, then on July 7, 1937 Japan entered into the war against China, and Kato was assigned to the Northern China area as a combat pilot and commander of the 1st *Chutai* of the 2nd Pursuit *Sentai*. Flying a Kawasaki Ki.10 Type 95 (Perry), Kato initiated the red hawk symbol that was to become his personal insignia during his combat career, and was destined to make him famous throughout Japan.

Recalled from China in June 1938 to attend the Army Military Staff College, Kato had led his fighter unit to over fifty aerial victories in the China campaign, accounting for at least eight of these himself. On July 15, 1938, while at the Staff College, Kato was promoted to the rank of Major. He graduated on March 9, 1939 and was made Inspector General of military education in Japan. Five months later he left Japan with General Terauchi

Close up detail of Kato's victory markings. Eagle in red symbolizes his wing. White half wings below represent victories.

A seated Kato reviews strategy with his wingman prior to a patrol in May, 1942.

to visit Germany and Italy. This trip was planned to cement relations with the Axis powers, as well as give Kato first hand knowledge of the aircraft development and training procedures of these countries.

Kato's return trip from this tour took him to the United States where he reviewed various new American aircraft designs and talked with key military personnel. He returned to Japan in his military staff position and remained there until April 10, 1941 when he was assigned as commander of the 64th Sentai in Canton, China. On December 8, 1941 (December 7th, American time), Japan attacked Pearl Harbor and Kato and his unit were posted to the Malaya area.

Participating in the air war in and around Malaya, Sumatra, Java, and Burma, the 64th ran up an impressive victory total of 268 enemy aircraft under Kato's command. Flying the Nakajima Ki.43 *"Hayabusa"* Type 1 fighter (Oscar), it is known that Kato made his presence felt among the Allied forces in the China-Burma Theater, both as an excellent combat pilot, a brilliant military tactician, and a leader who stressed the importance of teamwork.

On May 22, 1942 flying from his base near the Bay of Akyab, Burma, Kato took off to intercept a flight of Royal Air Force Blenheim fighter-bombers. In the ensuing dogfight, Kato destroyed one of the enemy aircraft, but was himself shot down. His plane crashed near a beach some 90 miles from his base.

Upon receiving word of Kato's death in Japan, the General Staff immediately promoted him to the posthumous rank of General in the Imperial Japanese Army. Considering his less than six month combat tenure, his 18+WWII victories were an incredible achievement.

One of the Ki.43 Oscars piloted by Kato as Sentai Commander of the 64th is illustrated on page 55.

Despite the fact that the Nakajima Ki 43 Oscar was, numerically, the most important Japanese Air Force fighter of WW II, only 40 were operational when war broke out. Brilliantly maneuverable, but comparatively slow, lightly armed and very vulnerable to machine gun fire, Oscar was kept in production throughout the war. Shown here a later model Ki.43 IIa.

Left Side
Only

Major Robin Olds
P-51D Wattisham, England
Spring, 1945

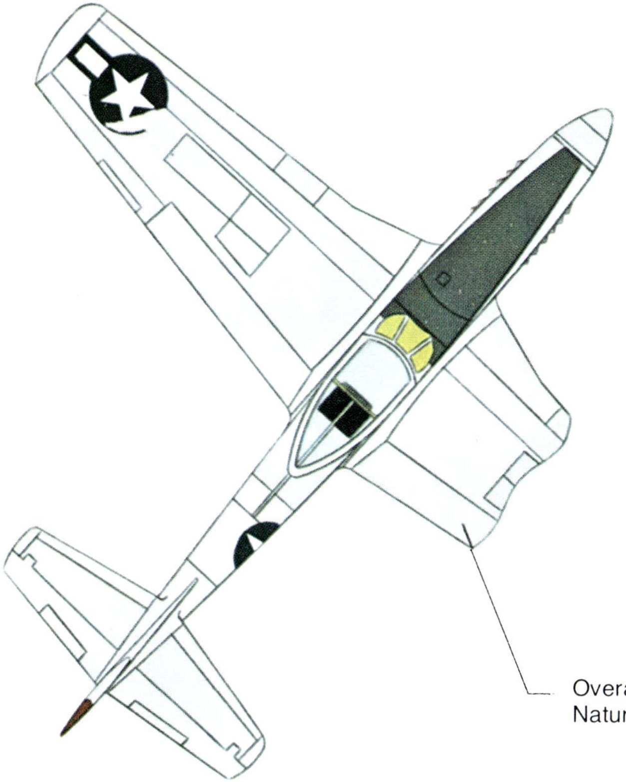

Overall Finish
Natural Metal

Personal Marking
Left Side Only

Major Günther Rall
Me 109G JG 52
Russia May, 1943

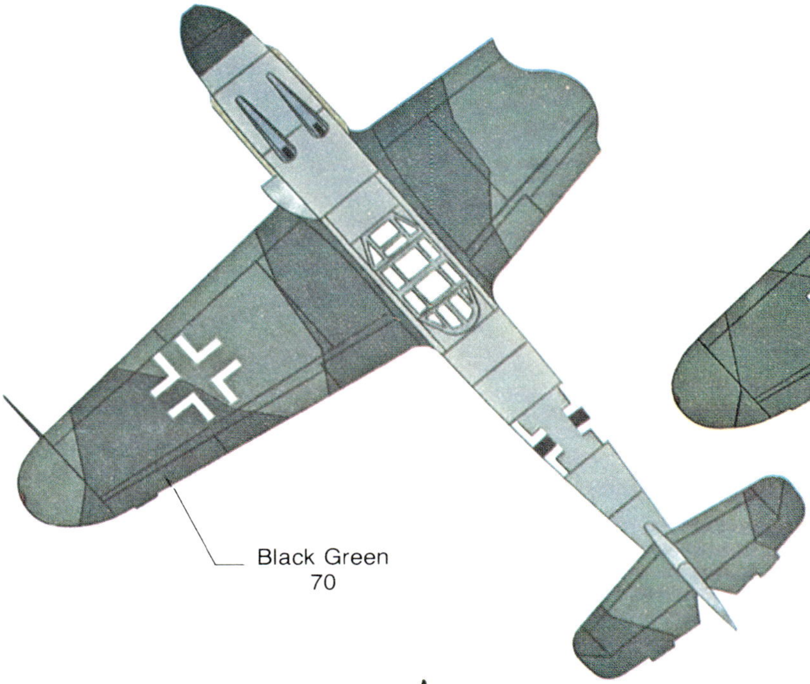

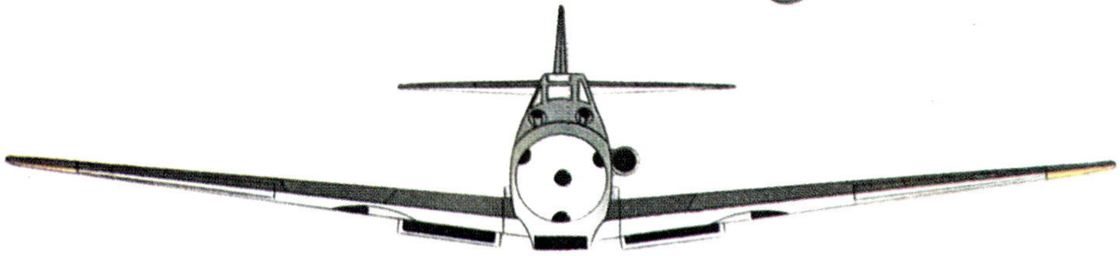

Major Wilhelm Batz
Me 109G-4
Southern Russia
January, 1943

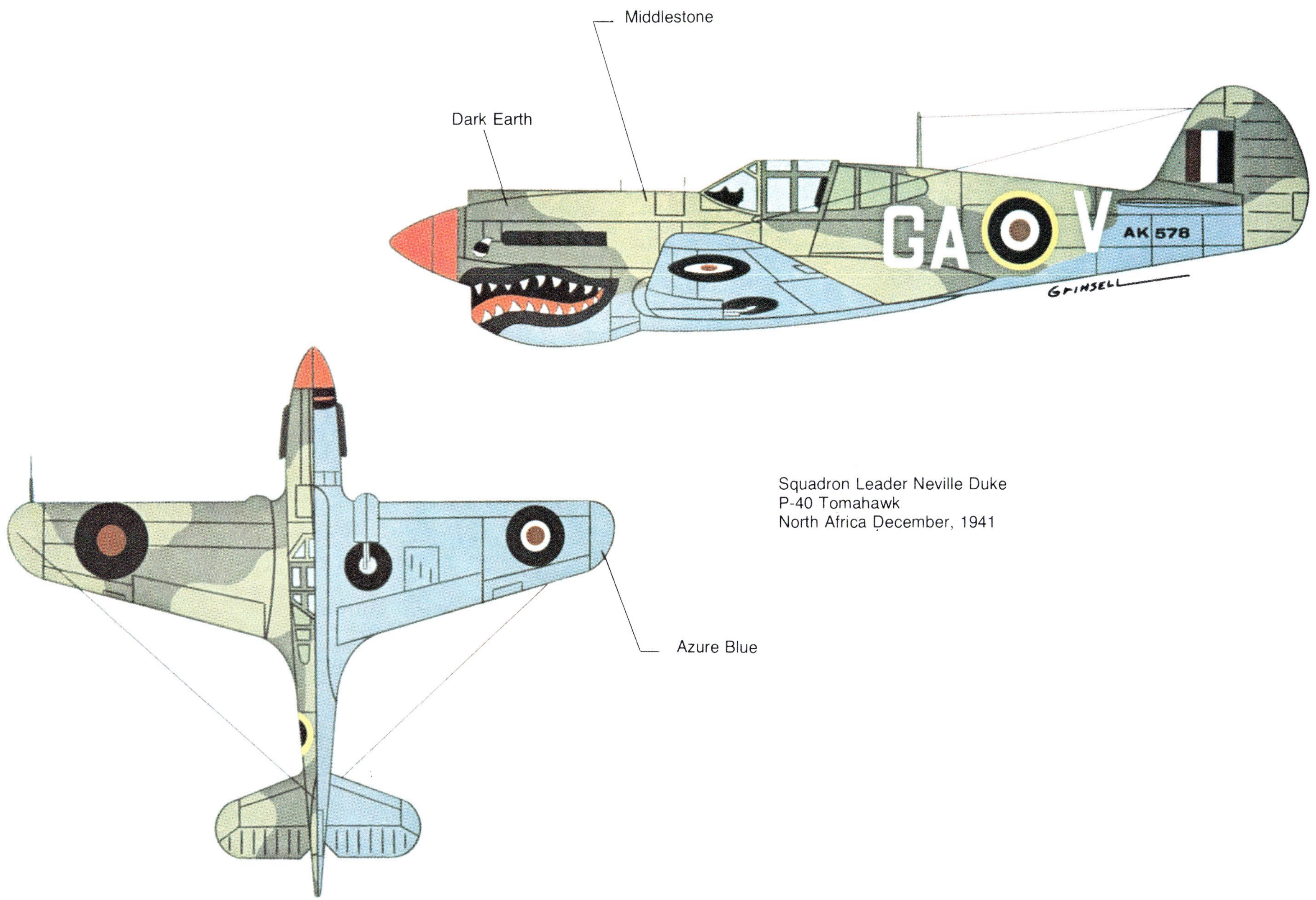

Squadron Leader Neville Duke
P-40 Tomahawk
North Africa December, 1941

Lt. Francis M. Fleming
F6F-3 USS Lexington
December 1943

Insignia of VF-16

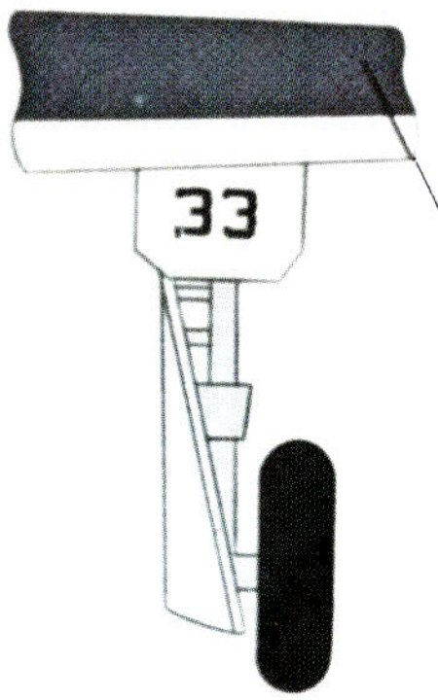

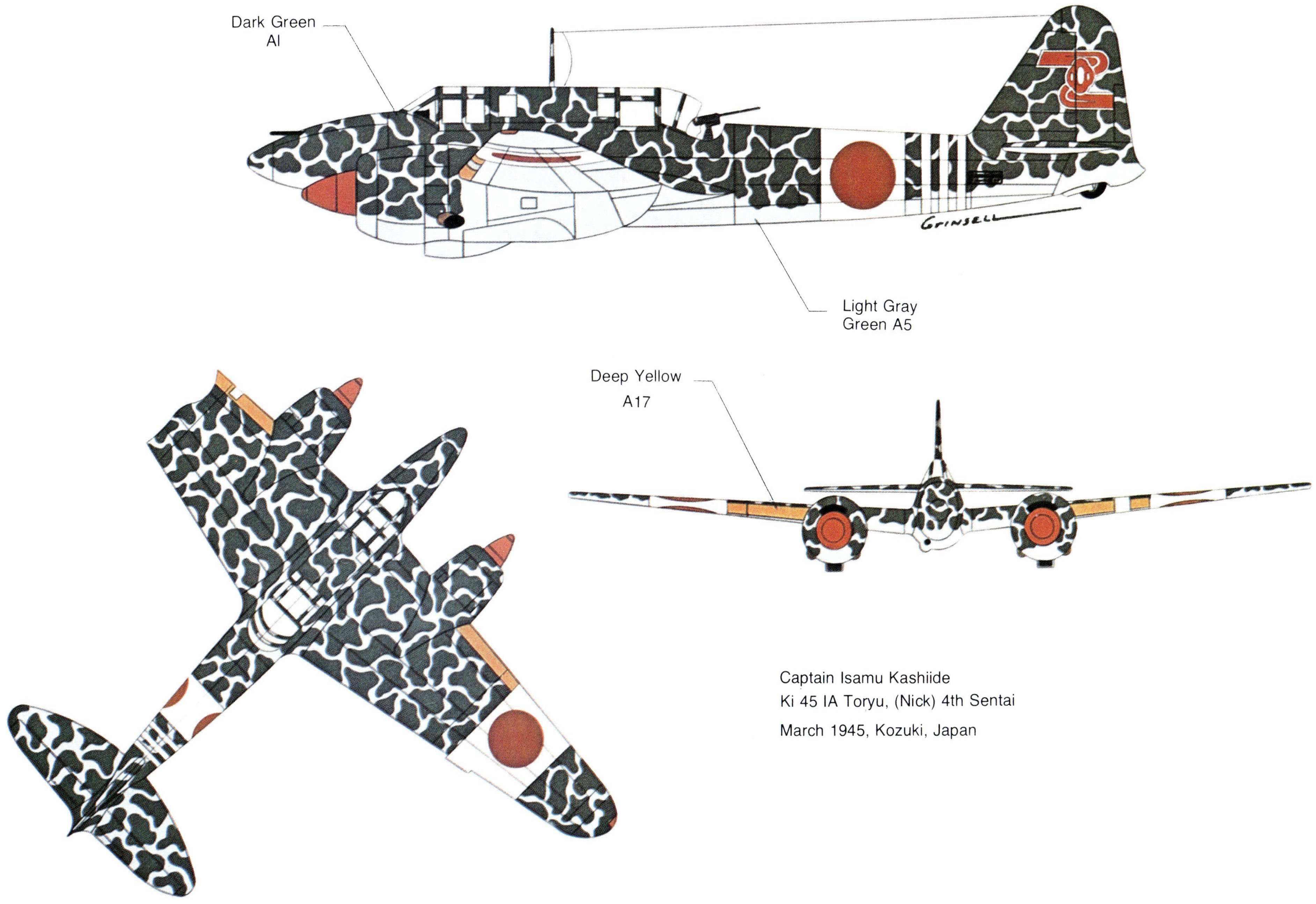

Captain Isamu Kashiide
Ki 45 IA Toryu, (Nick) 4th Sentai
March 1945, Kozuki, Japan

Glossy Sea Blue
FS 595-15042

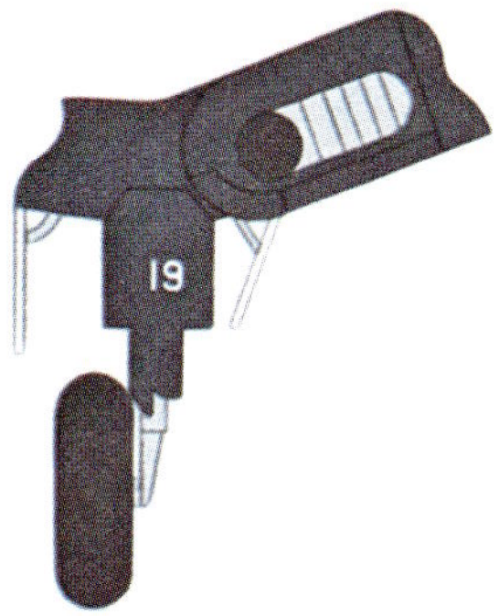

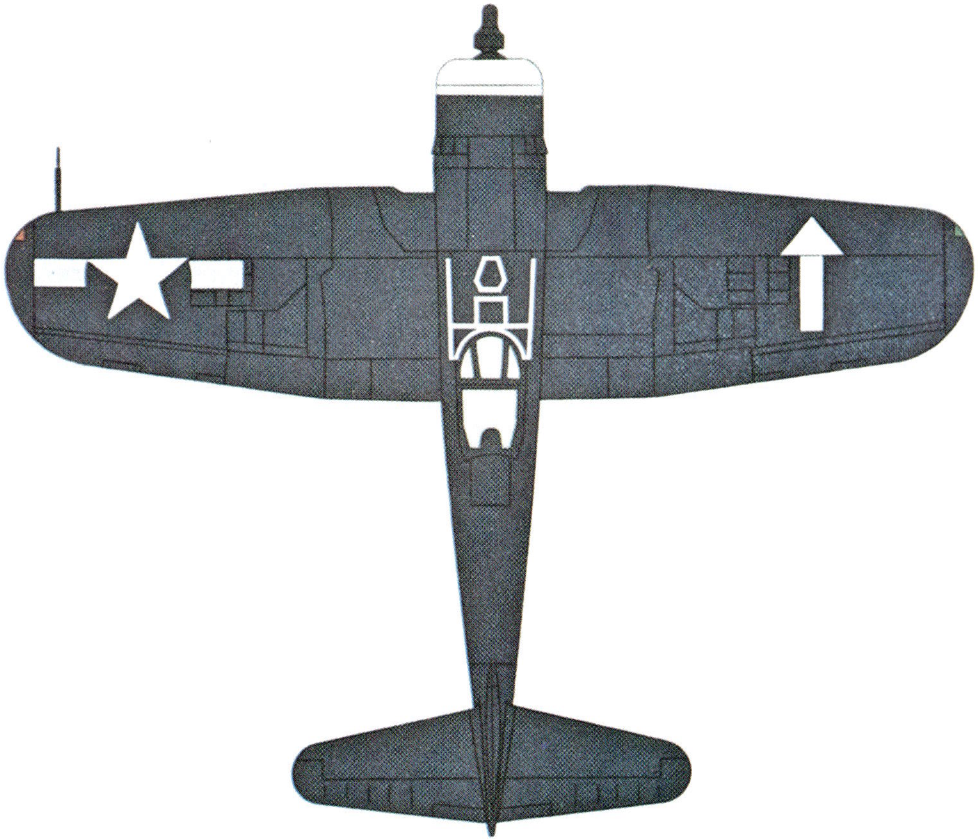

Major Archie Donahue
F4U-1D VMF-451
USS Bunker Hill March, 1945

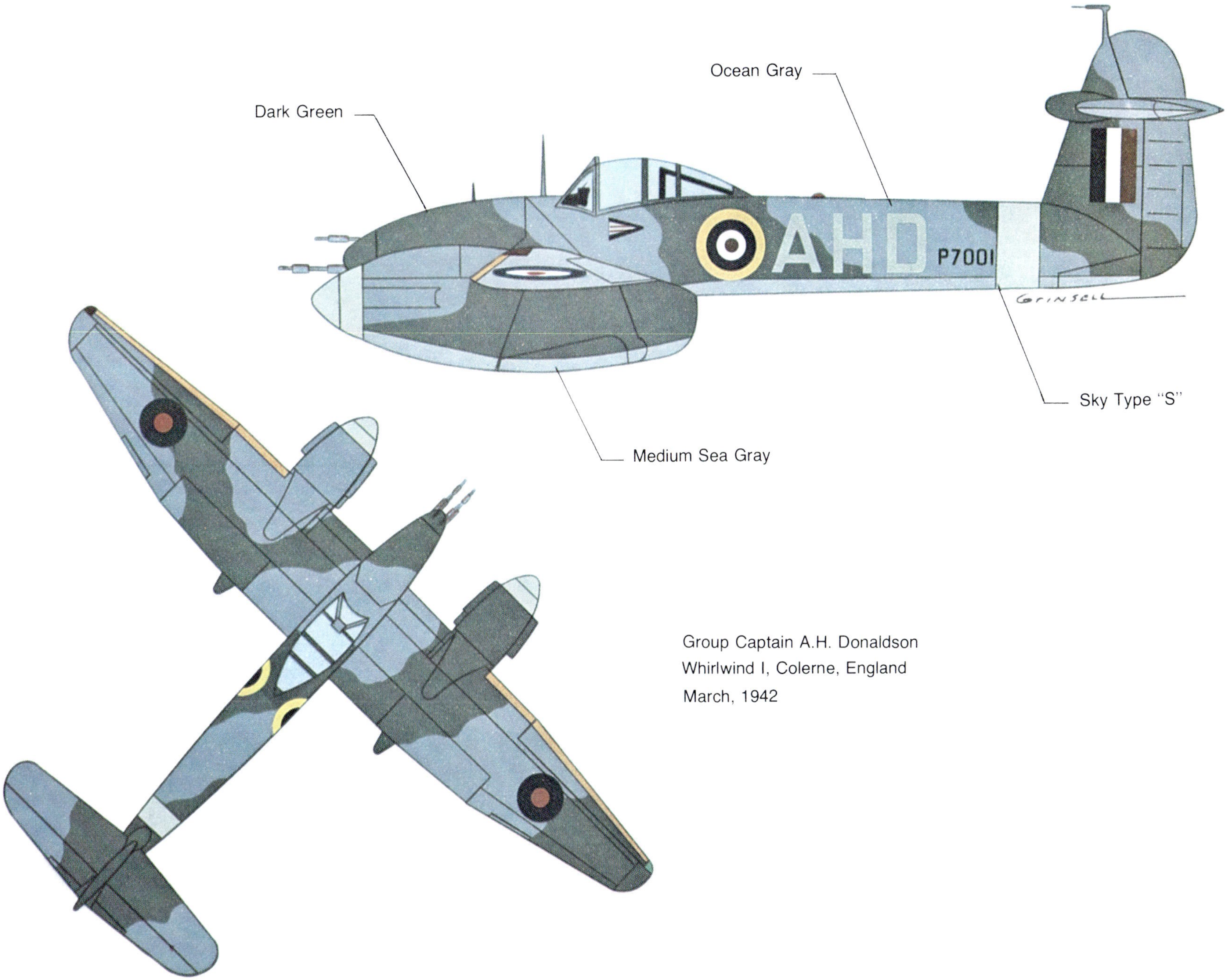

Group Captain A.H. Donaldson
Whirlwind I, Colerne, England
March, 1942

Colonel David Schilling
P-47D-1-RE
Halesworth, England
September, 1943

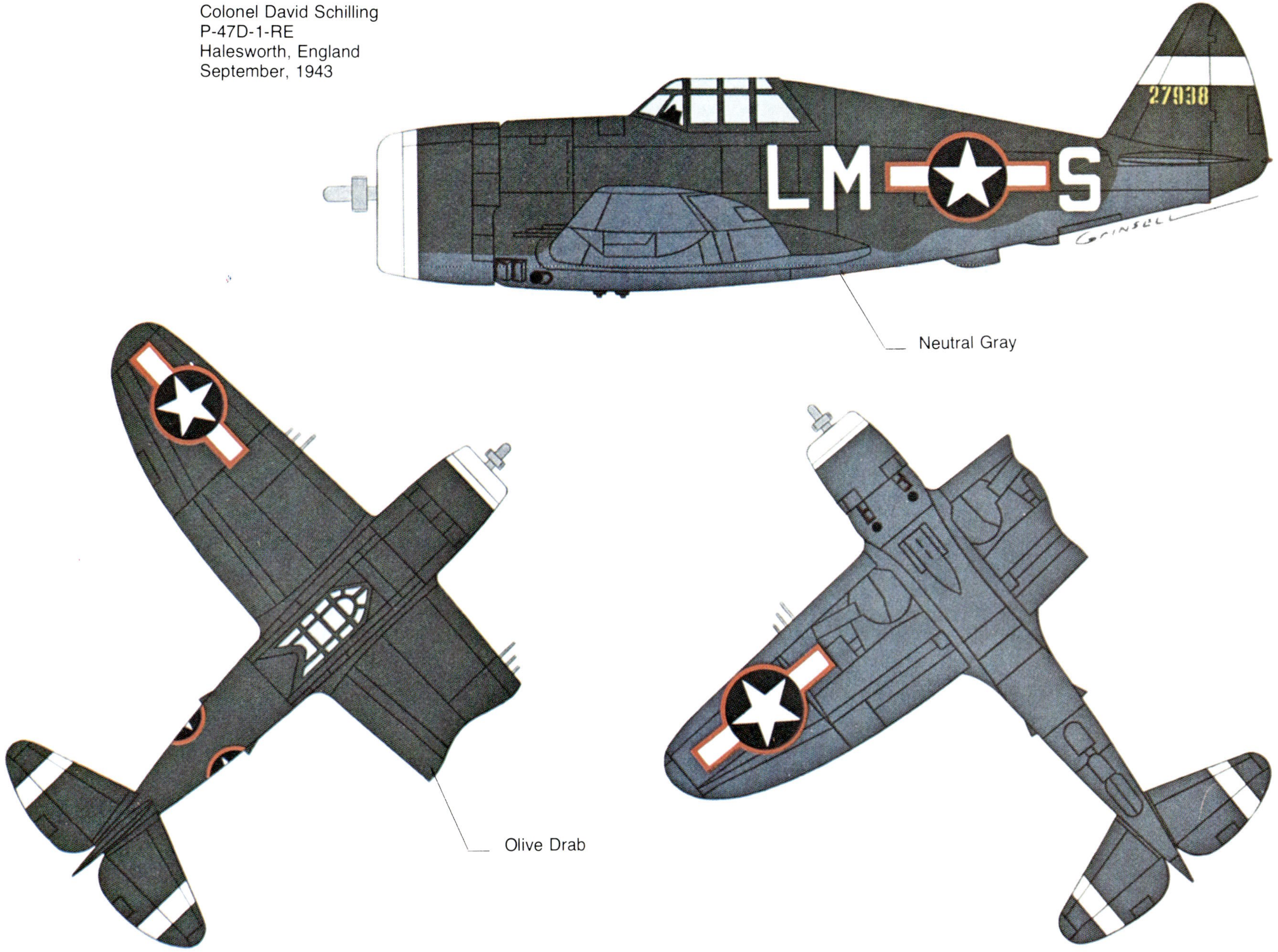

Me 109E-4
flown by Colonel Adolf Galland
Kommodore (Wing Commander) JG 26
France, November, 1940

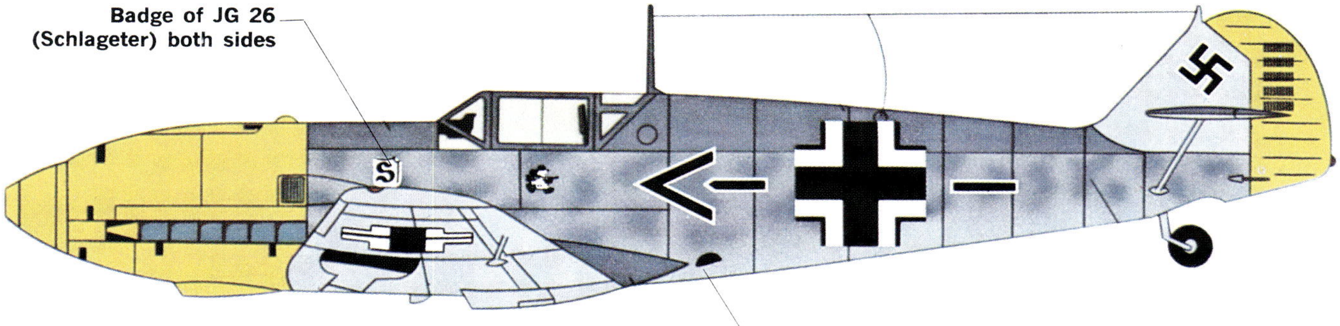

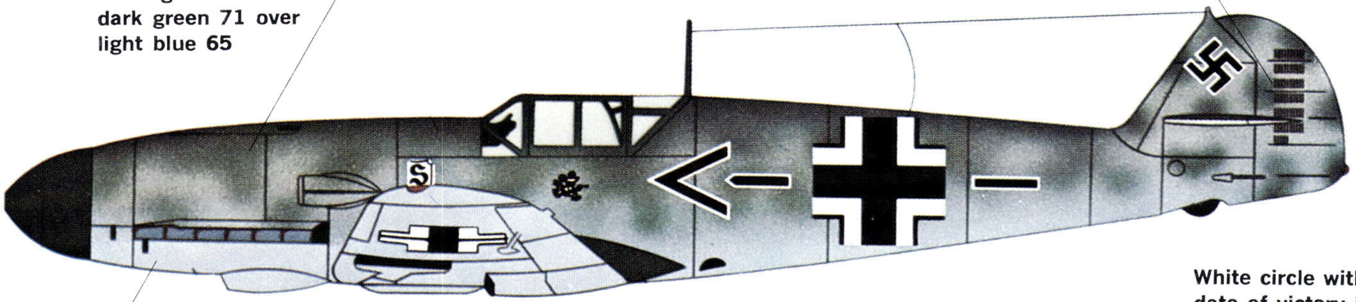

Me 109F-2
flown by Colonel Galland
JG 26
France, June, 1941
*Galland was shot down by
a Spitfire in this machine

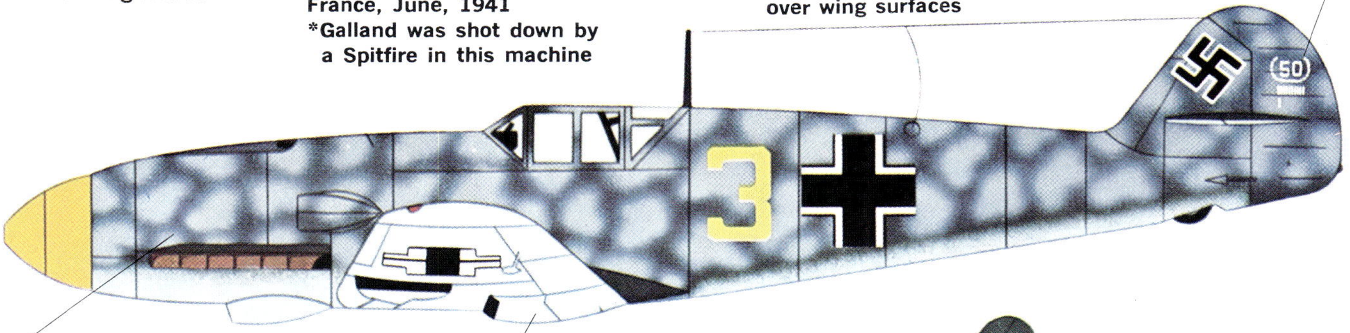

Me 109G-2
flown by Lt. Herbert Kaiser
II/JG 77
Italy, January, 1944

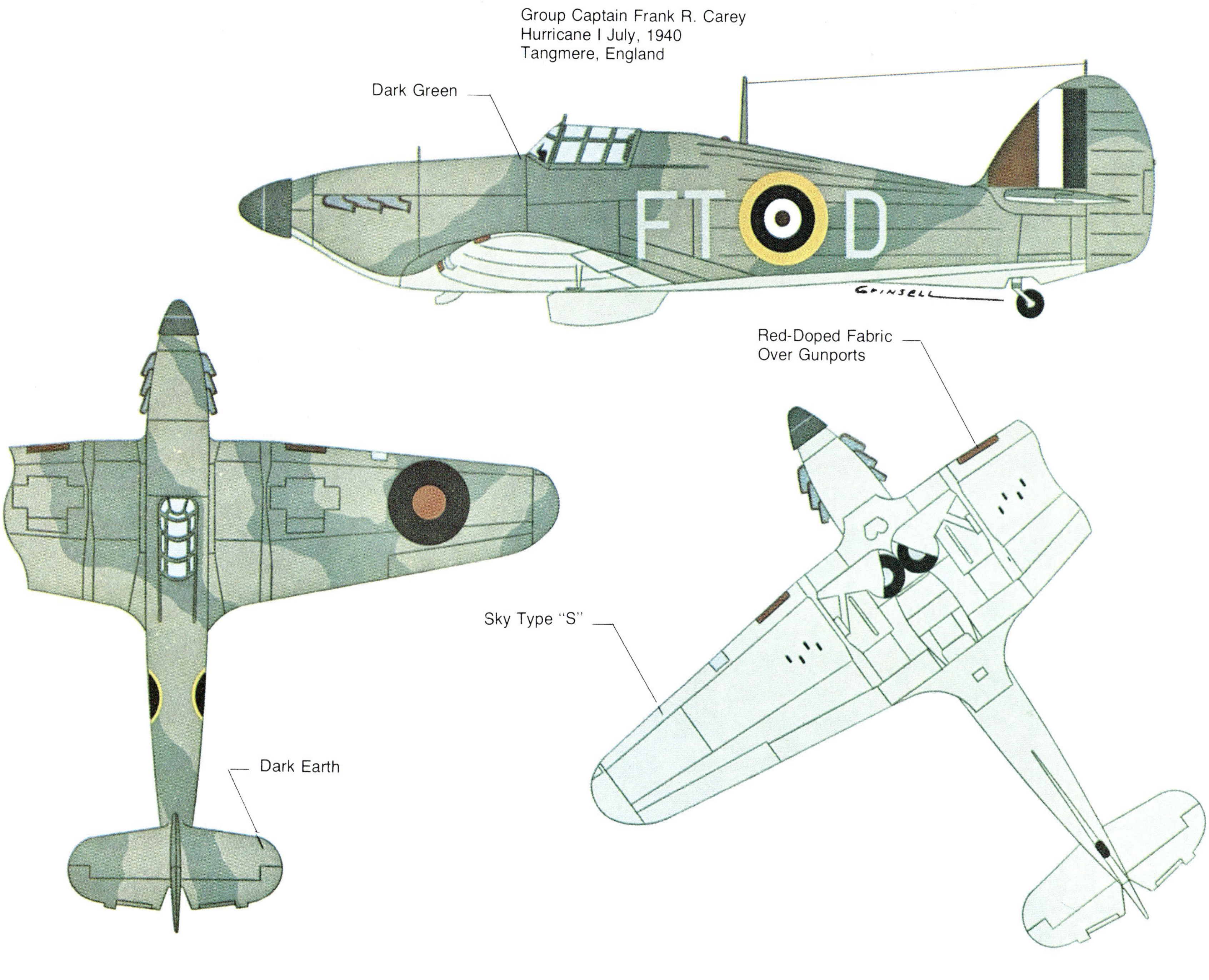
Group Captain Frank R. Carey
Hurricane I July, 1940
Tangmere, England
Dark Green
FT D
GRINSELL
Red-Doped Fabric Over Gunports
Sky Type "S"
Dark Earth

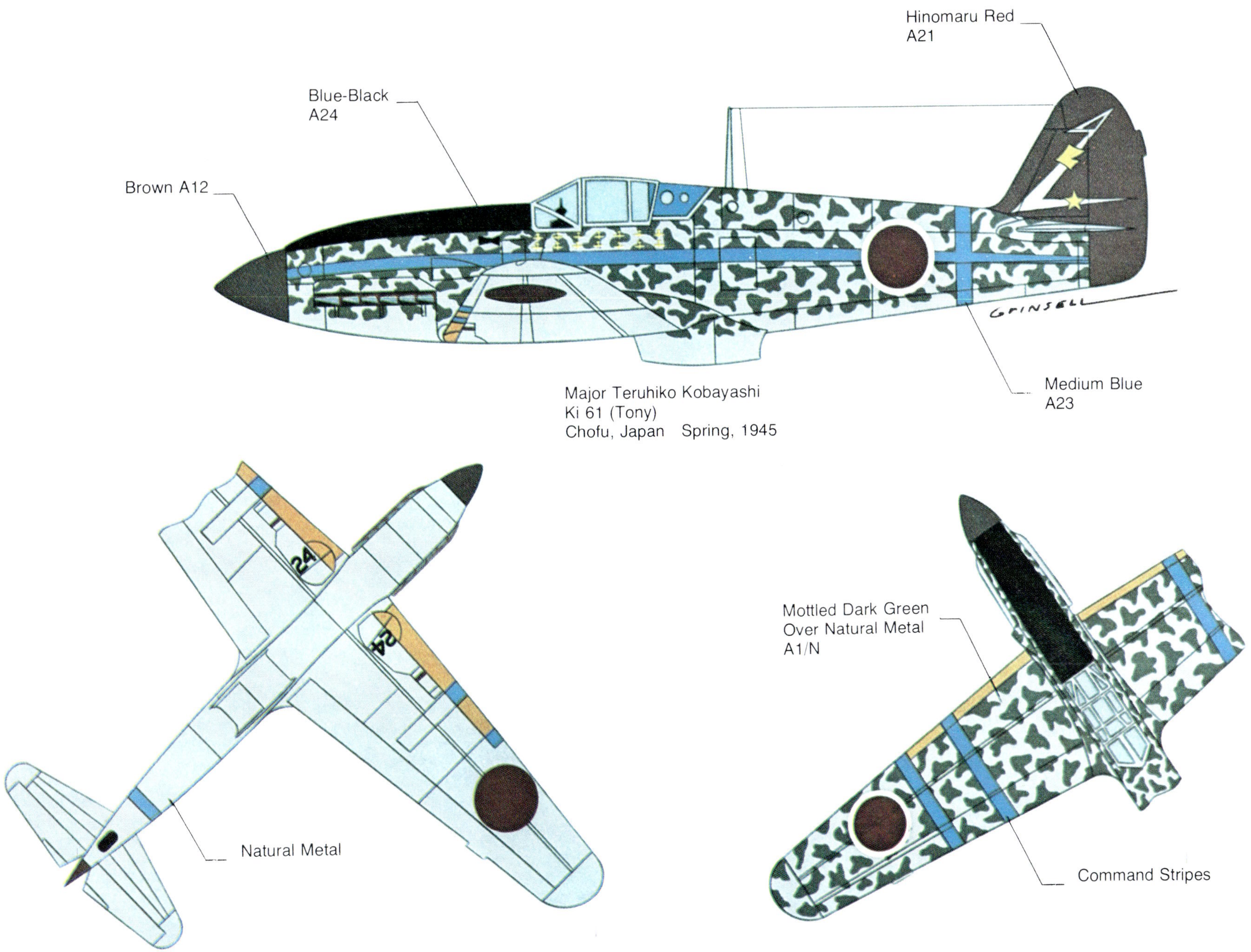

Major Teruhiko Kobayashi
Ki 61 (Tony)
Chofu, Japan Spring, 1945

sand yellow 79

Insignia of
JG 27
both sides

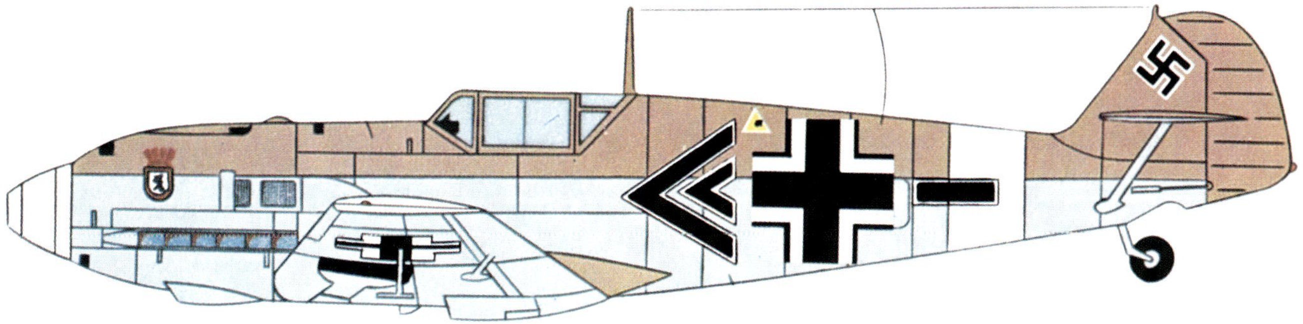

Me 109E-4N/Trop.
flown by Colonel Gustav Rodel
Group Commander II/JG 27
Libya, summer 1941

light blue 65

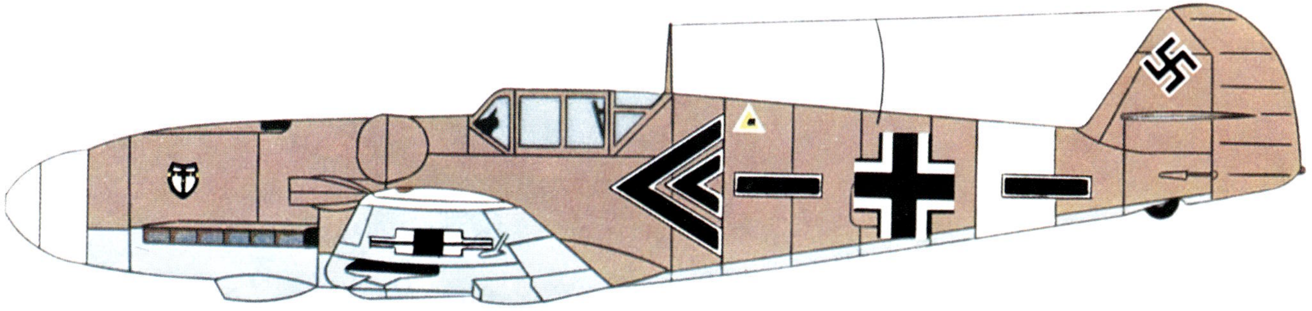

Insignia of
JG 27
both sides

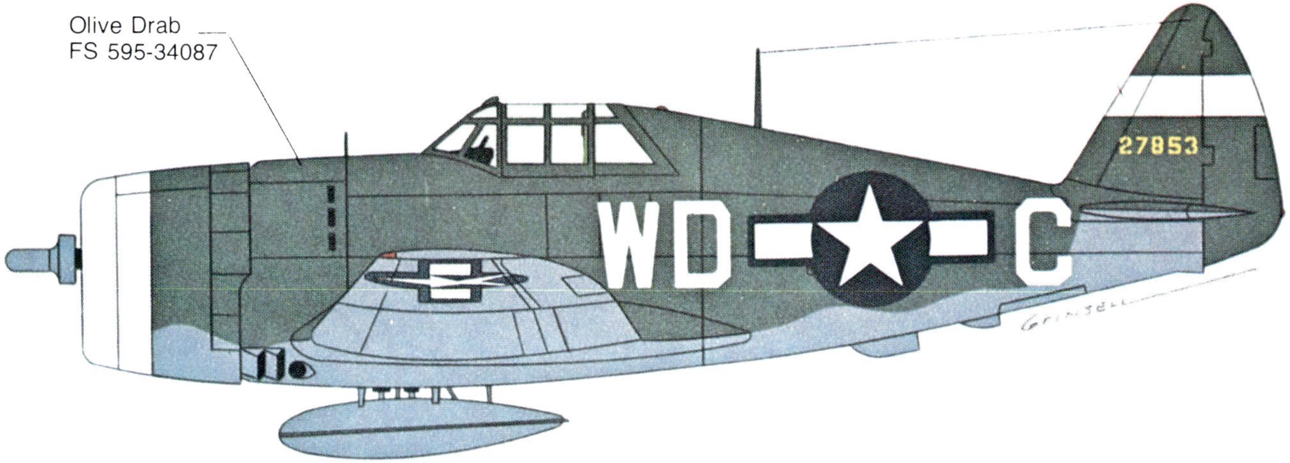

Colonel Donald Blakeslee
P-47D-1RE 4th Fighter Group

Debden, England August, 1943

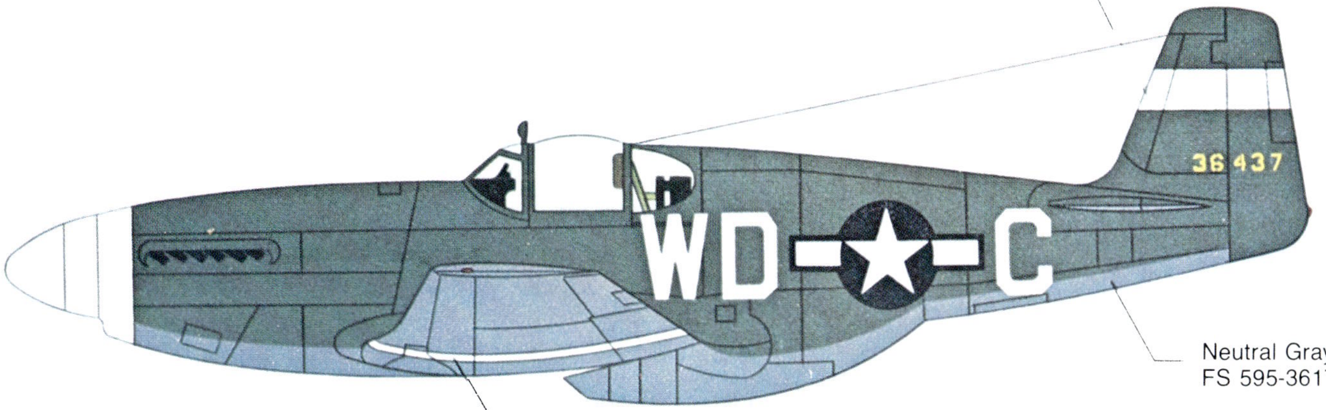

P-51B-5 4th Fighter Group
Debden, England, March, 1944

Me 109G-4
flown by Lt. Hans-Joachim Kroschinski
Russia, December, 1942

Insignia of JG 54
both sides

Insignia of
II/JG 27
both sides

Me 109G-2
Lt. Kroschinski
Russia, August, 1942

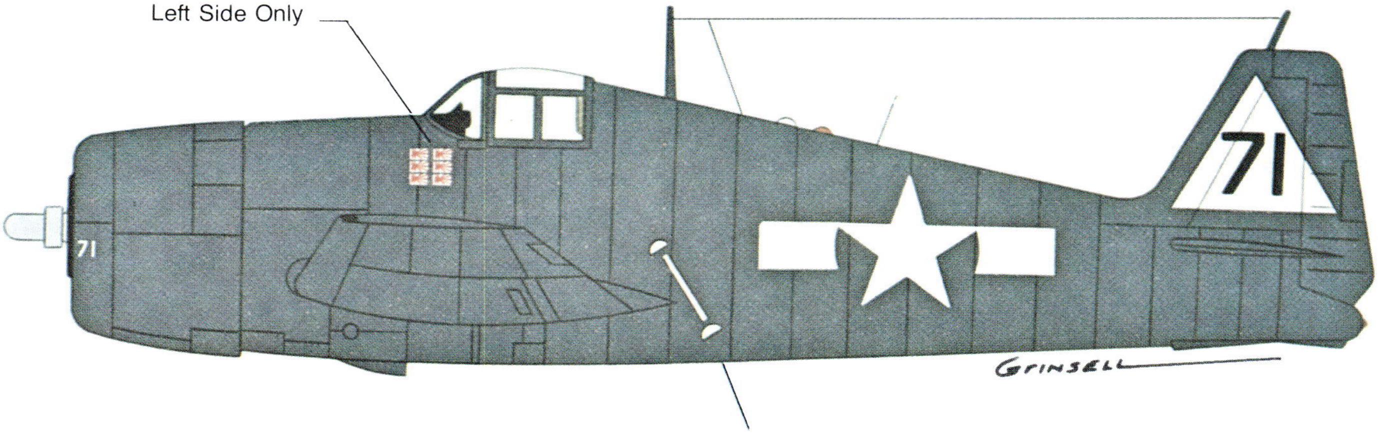

Lt. Leo McCuddin
F6F-5 Hellcat
USS Enterprise   November, 1944

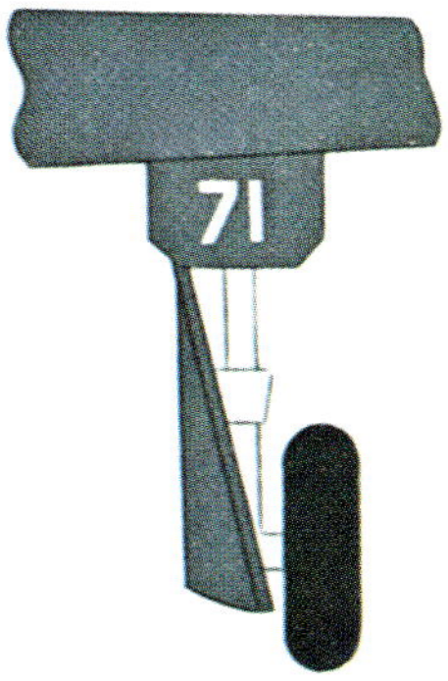

Insignia of VF-20
(not carried on aircraft)

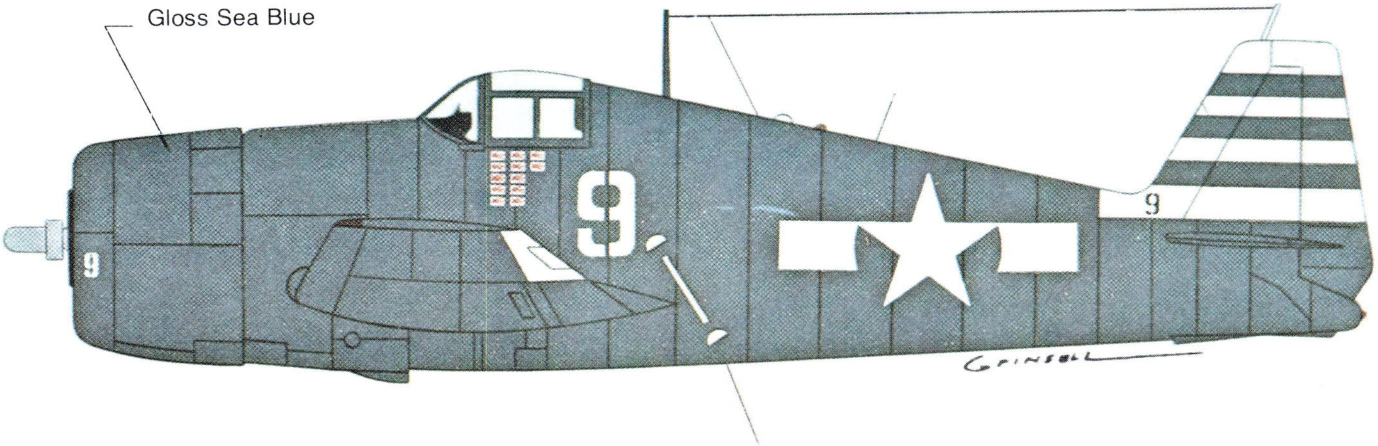

Lt. Cmdr. Hamilton McWhorter
F6F Hellcat
USS Randolph   February, 1945

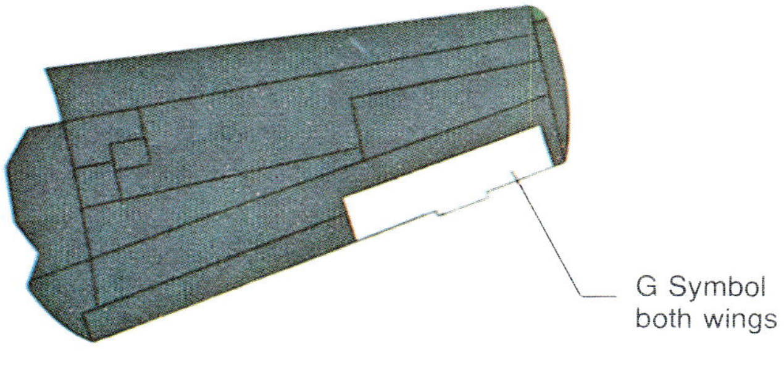

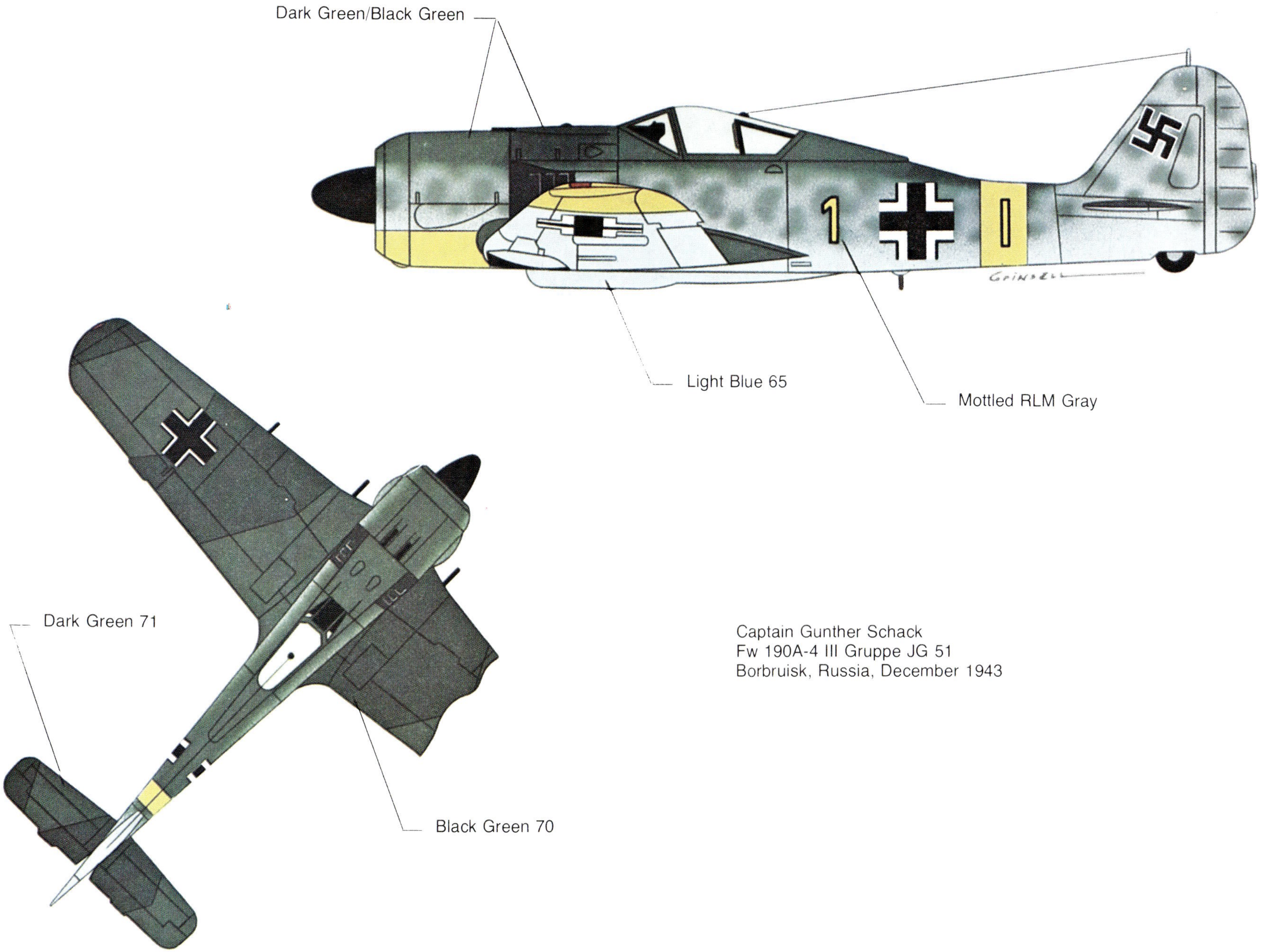

Captain Gunther Schack
Fw 190A-4 III Gruppe JG 51
Borbruisk, Russia, December 1943

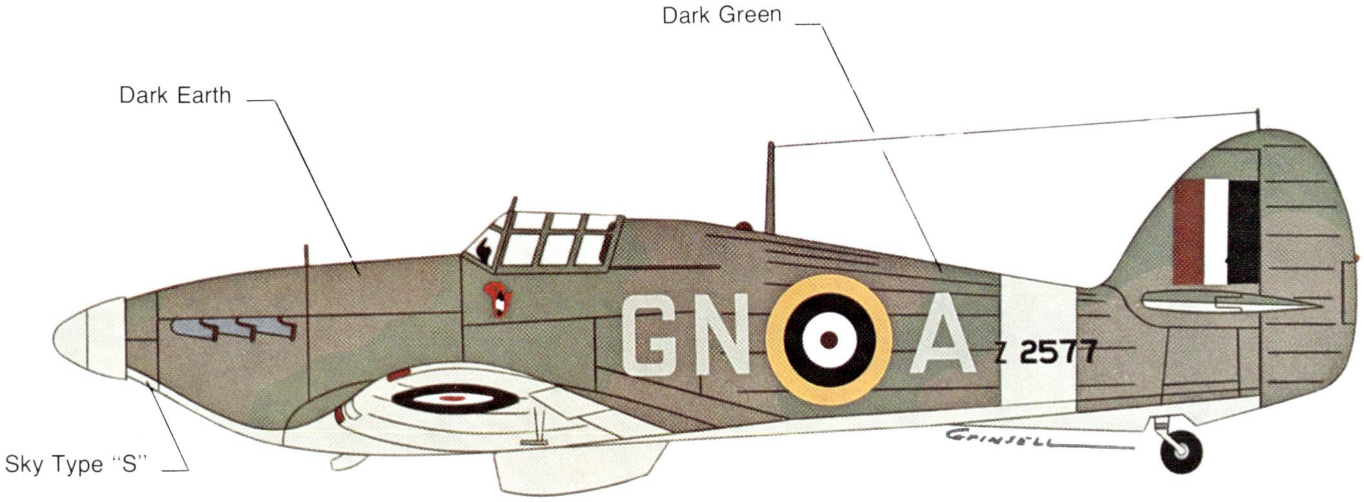

Squadron Leader Albert G. Lewis
Hurricane I
North Weald, England,
May, 1941

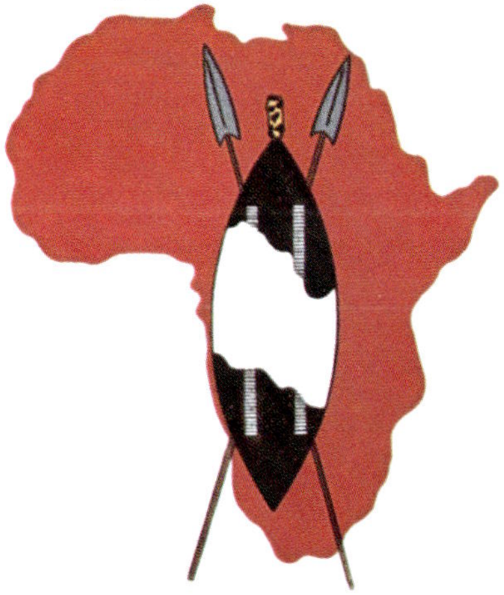

Personal Emblem
left side only

P-38L
Flown by Major Thomas McGuire
Philippines, January, 1945

left side only

nose emblem detail

fuselage detail

natural metal overall

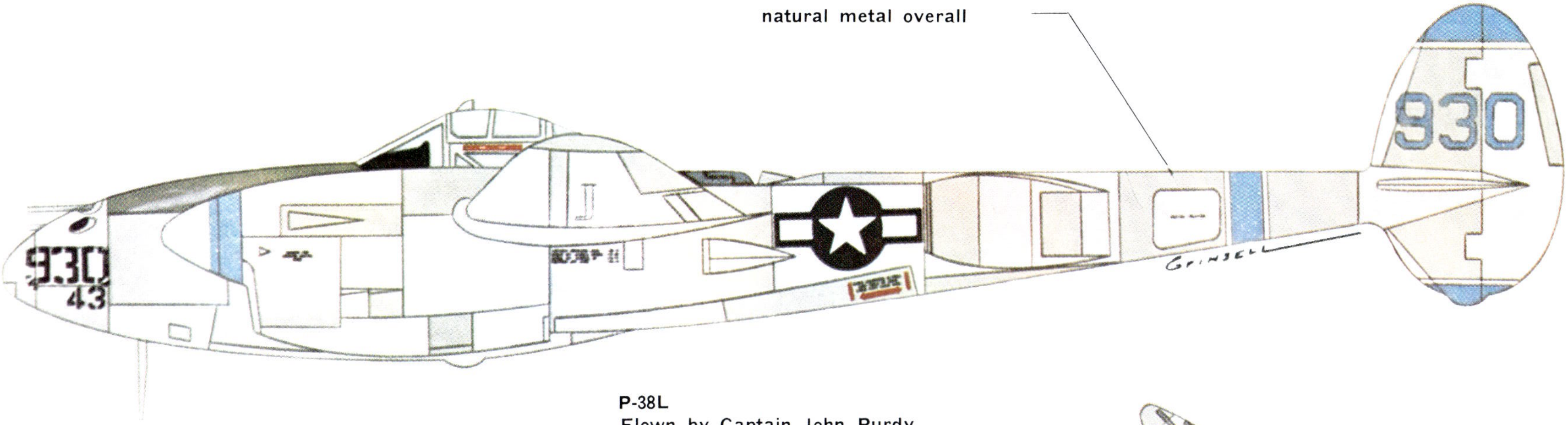

P-38L
Flown by Captain John Purdy
New Guinea, December, 1944

right side

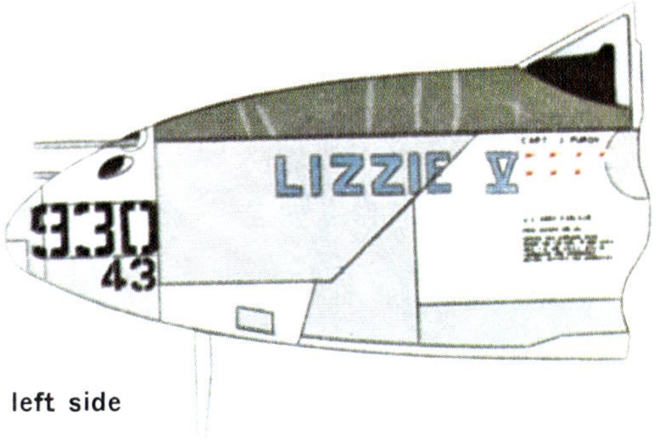

left side

Insignia of JG 77
"Herzas" both sides

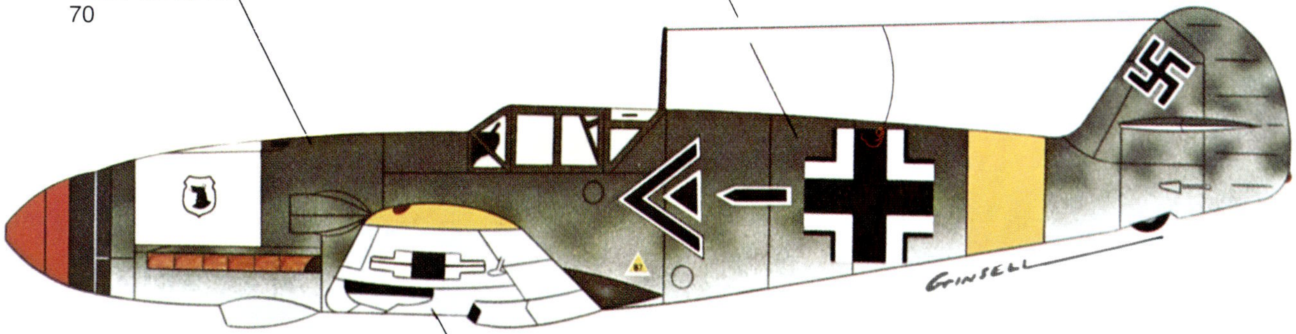

Colonel Johannes Steinhoff
Me 109F-4 JG 77
Russia January, 1943

Unit Insignia of JG 52
both sides

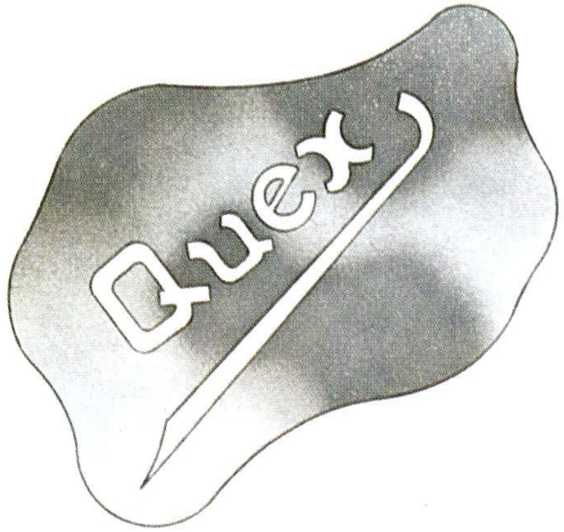

Personal Marking
left side only

Lt. Walter Wolfrum
Me 109G-6 Russia, April, 1944

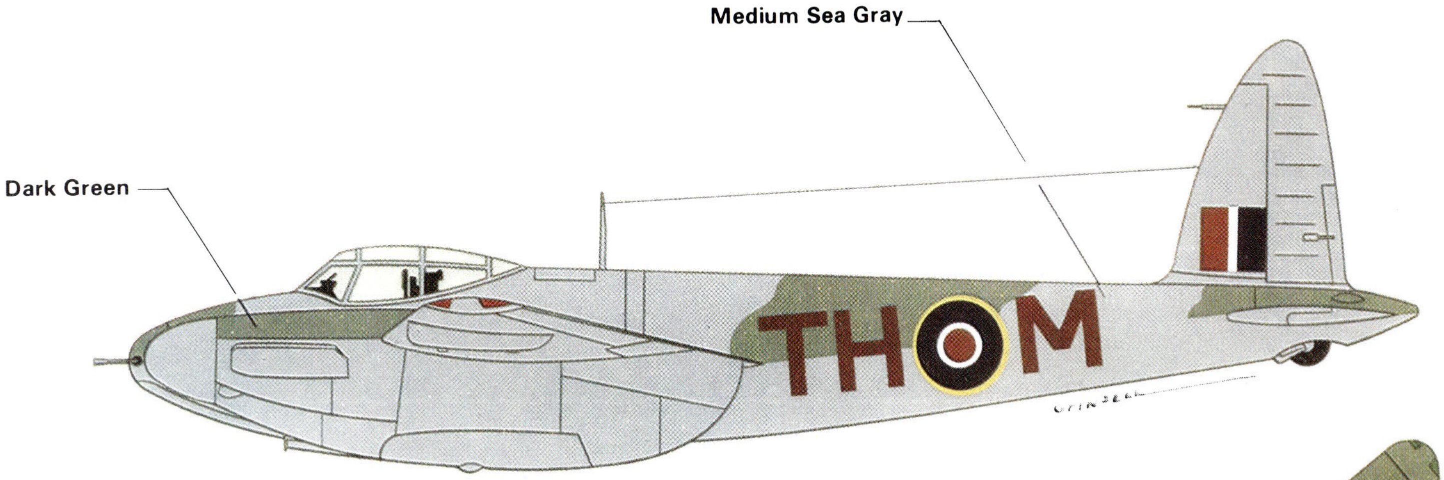

Mosquito VI "Black Rufe"
Hunsdon, Hertfordshire,
England
flown by Squadron Leader
Robert Kipp
418 Squadron
October, 1944

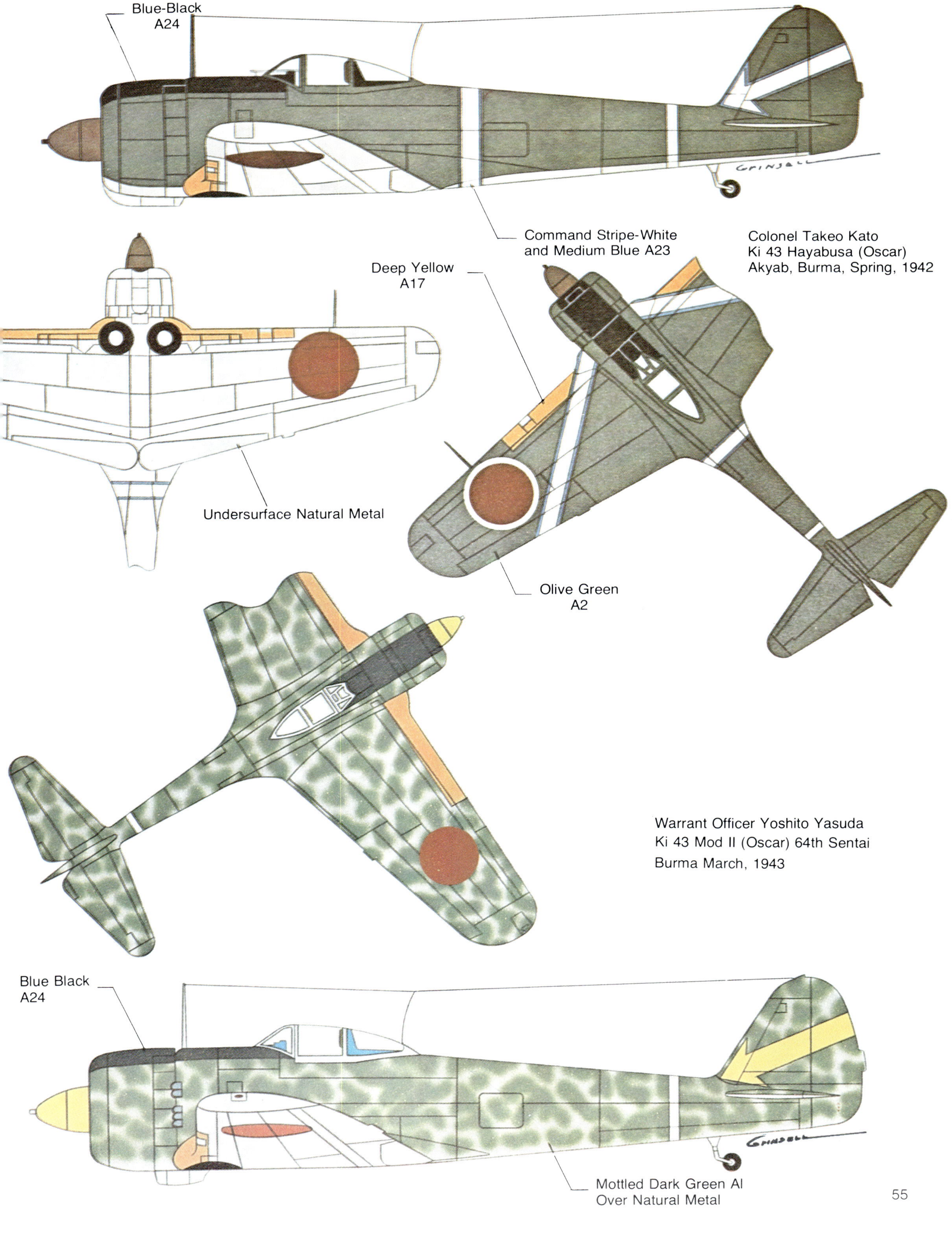

Colonel Takeo Kato
Ki 43 Hayabusa (Oscar)
Akyab, Burma, Spring, 1942

Warrant Officer Yoshito Yasuda
Ki 43 Mod II (Oscar) 64th Sentai
Burma March, 1943

Me 109G, Russia, February 1943

Major Hans "Assi" Hahn

Me 109F, France, Spring 1941

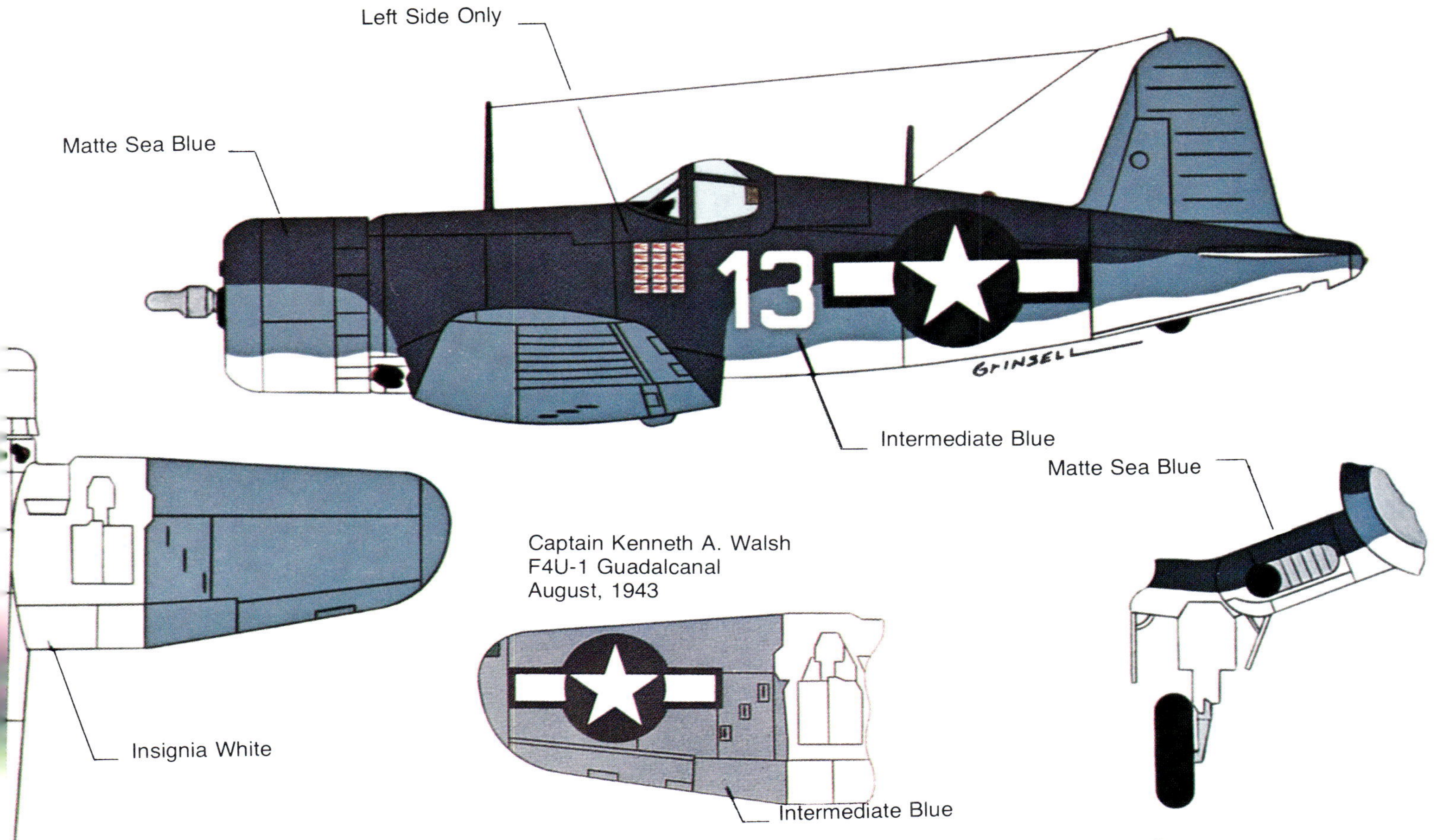

Captain Kenneth A. Walsh
F4U-1 Guadalcanal
August, 1943

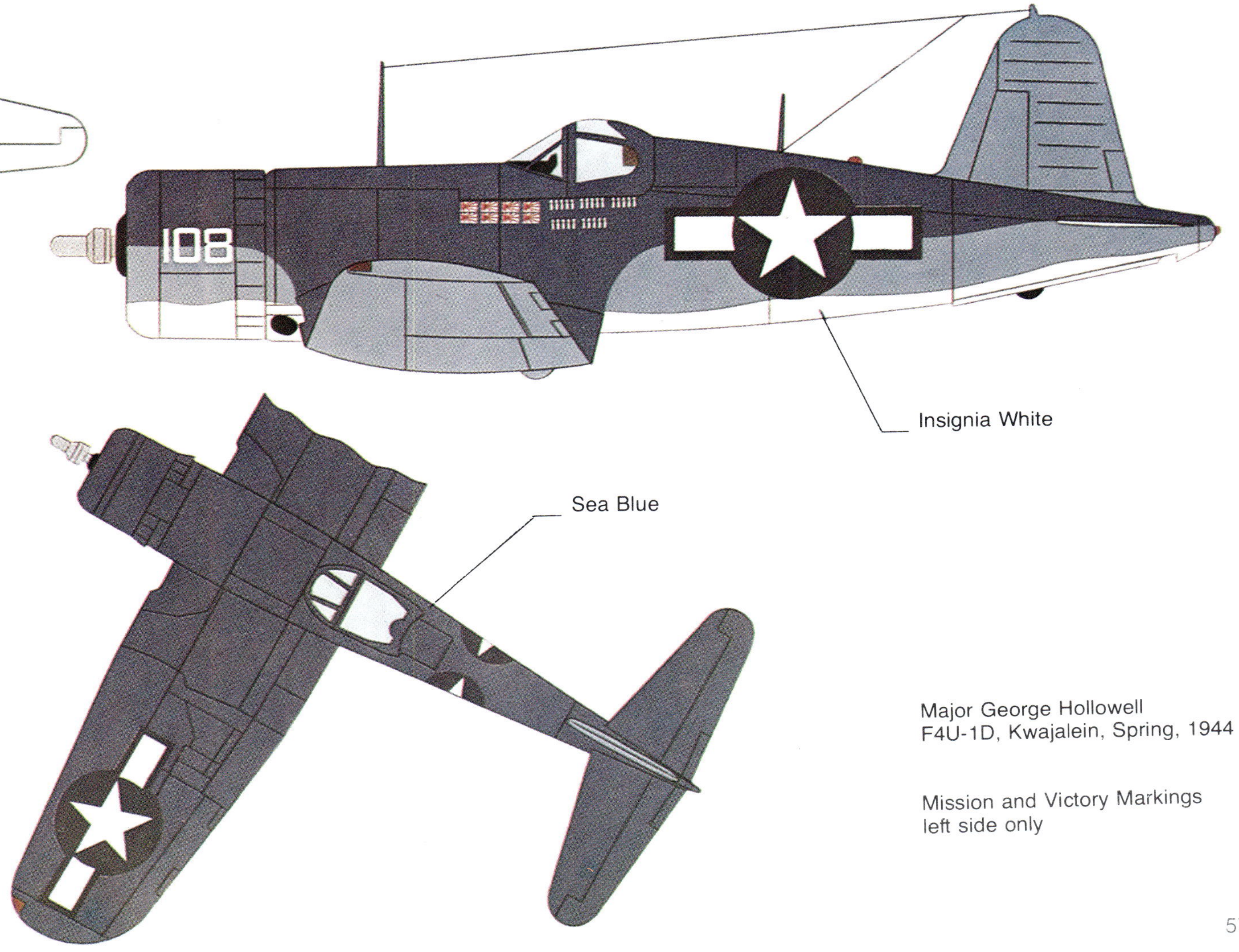

Major George Hollowell
F4U-1D, Kwajalein, Spring, 1944

Mission and Victory Markings
left side only

Recognition Bands On Upper And Lower Wings And Tail Surfaces

P-51D Martlesham Heath, England
November, 1944

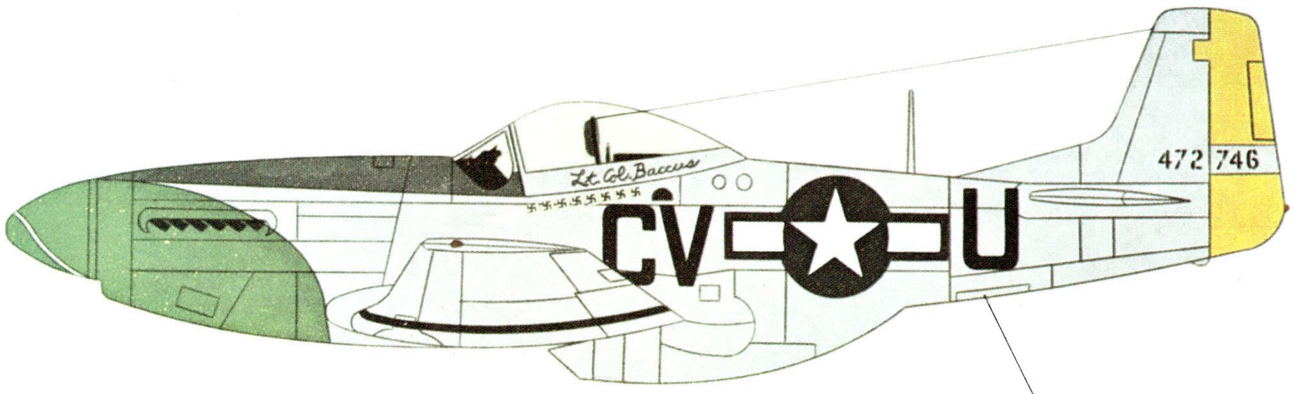

Victory Markings On Left Side Only

Lt. Colonel Donald A. Baccus
P-51D East Wretham, England
May, 1945

Overall Aircraft Natural Metal

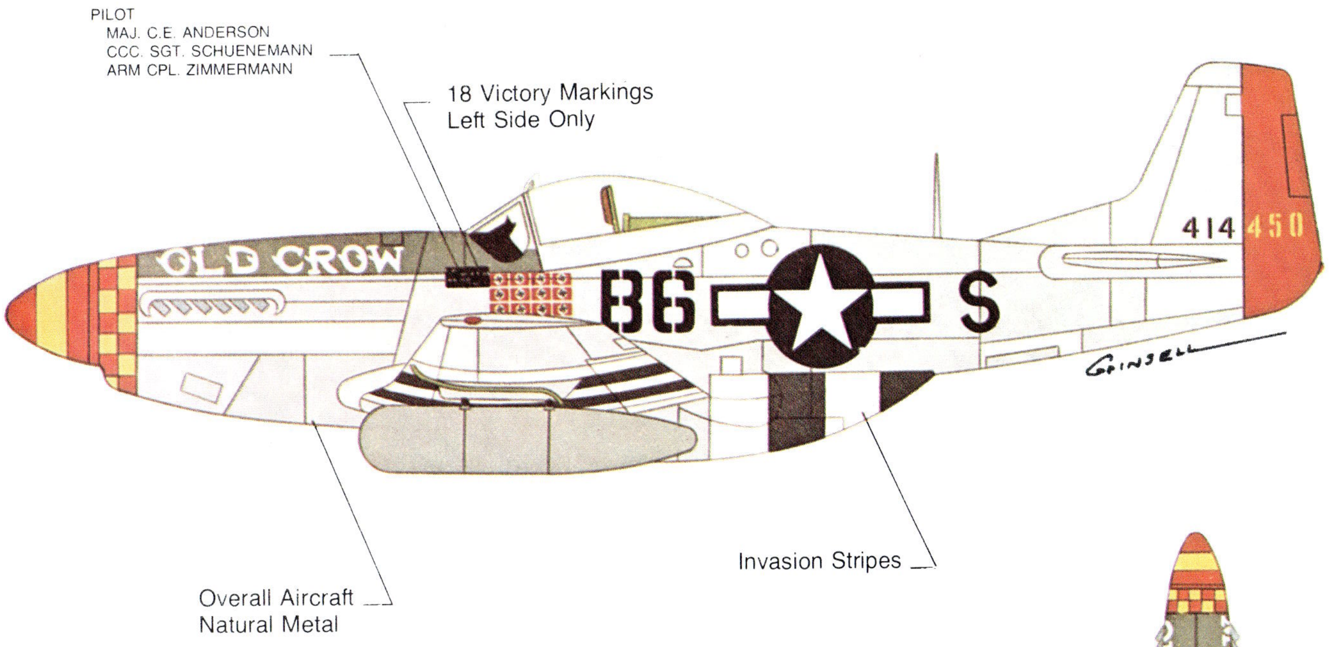

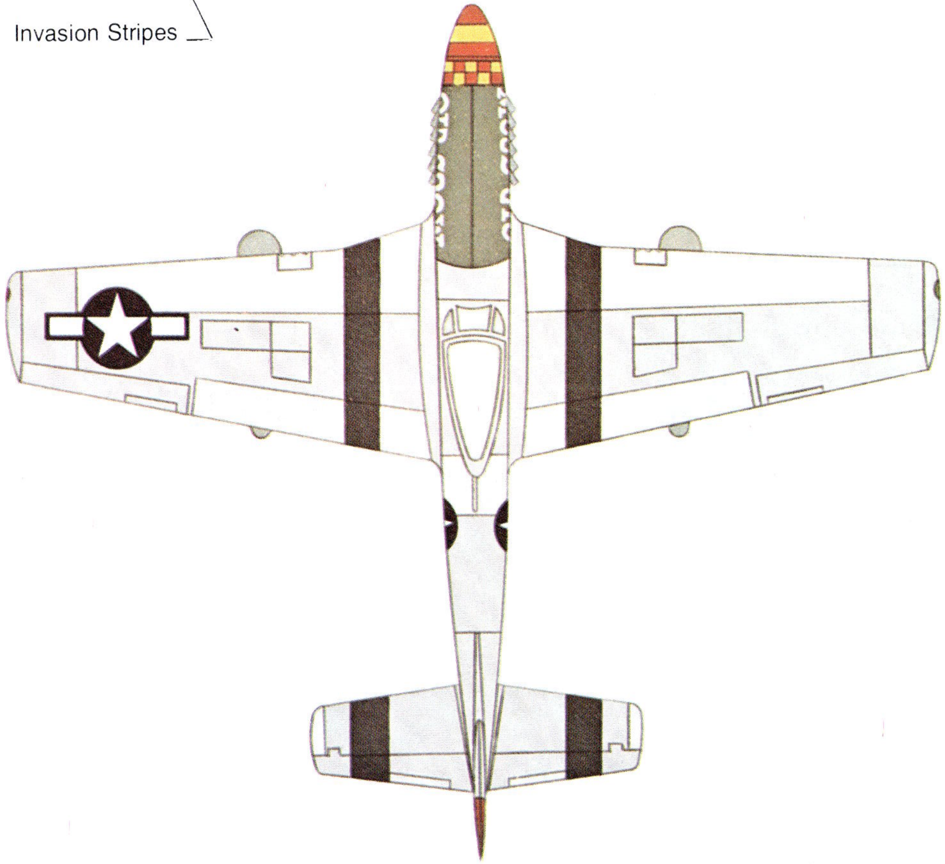

Major Clarence Anderson
P-51D 357th Fighter Group
Leiston, England Autumn, 1944

Major Wilhelm Hergert
Me 110G-4, Florennes, Belgium
December 1943   I Gruppe NJG 4

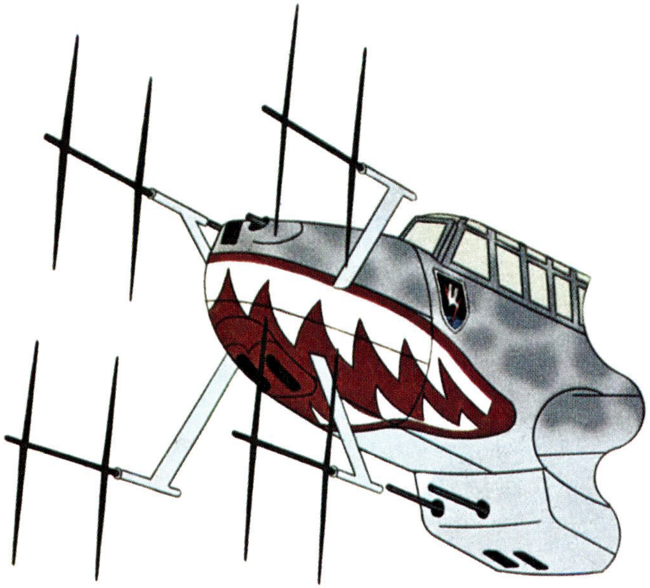

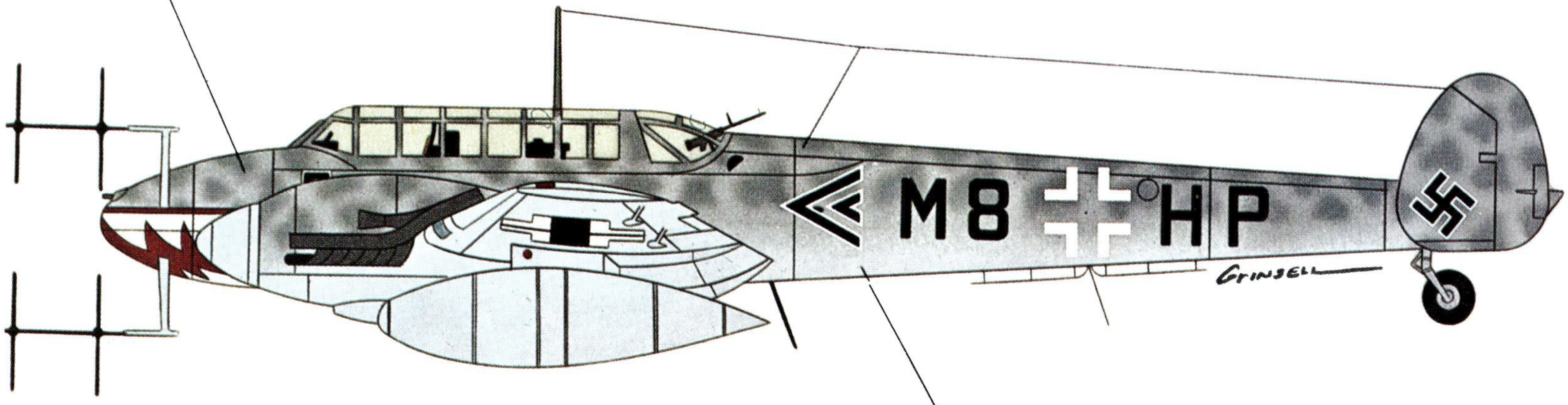

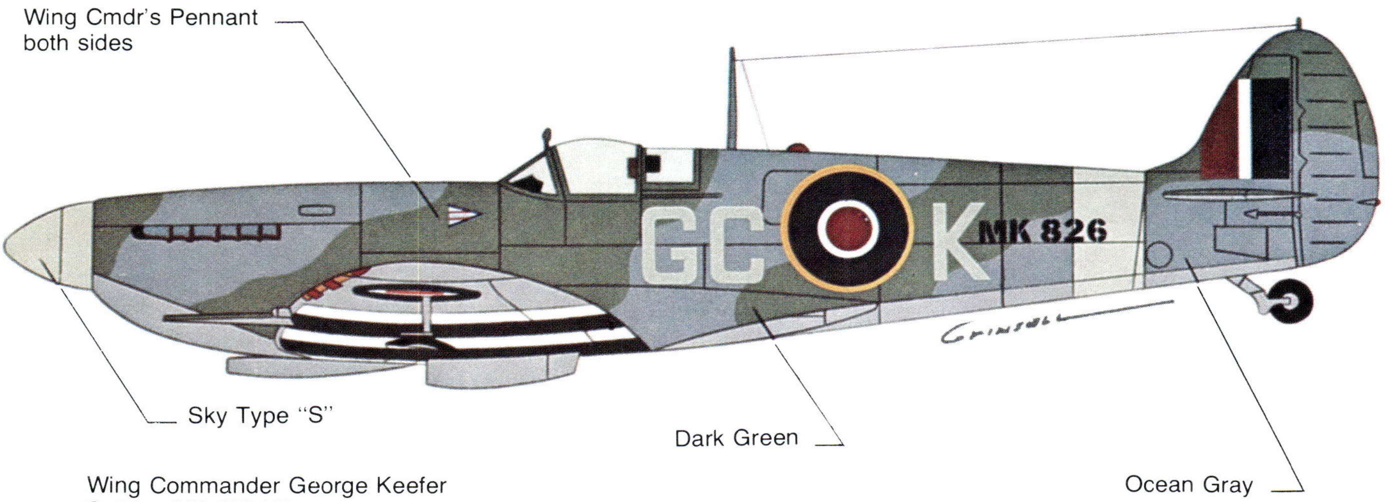

Wing Commander George Keefer
Spitfire IXB 126 Wing
Beny sur Mer, France
July, 1944

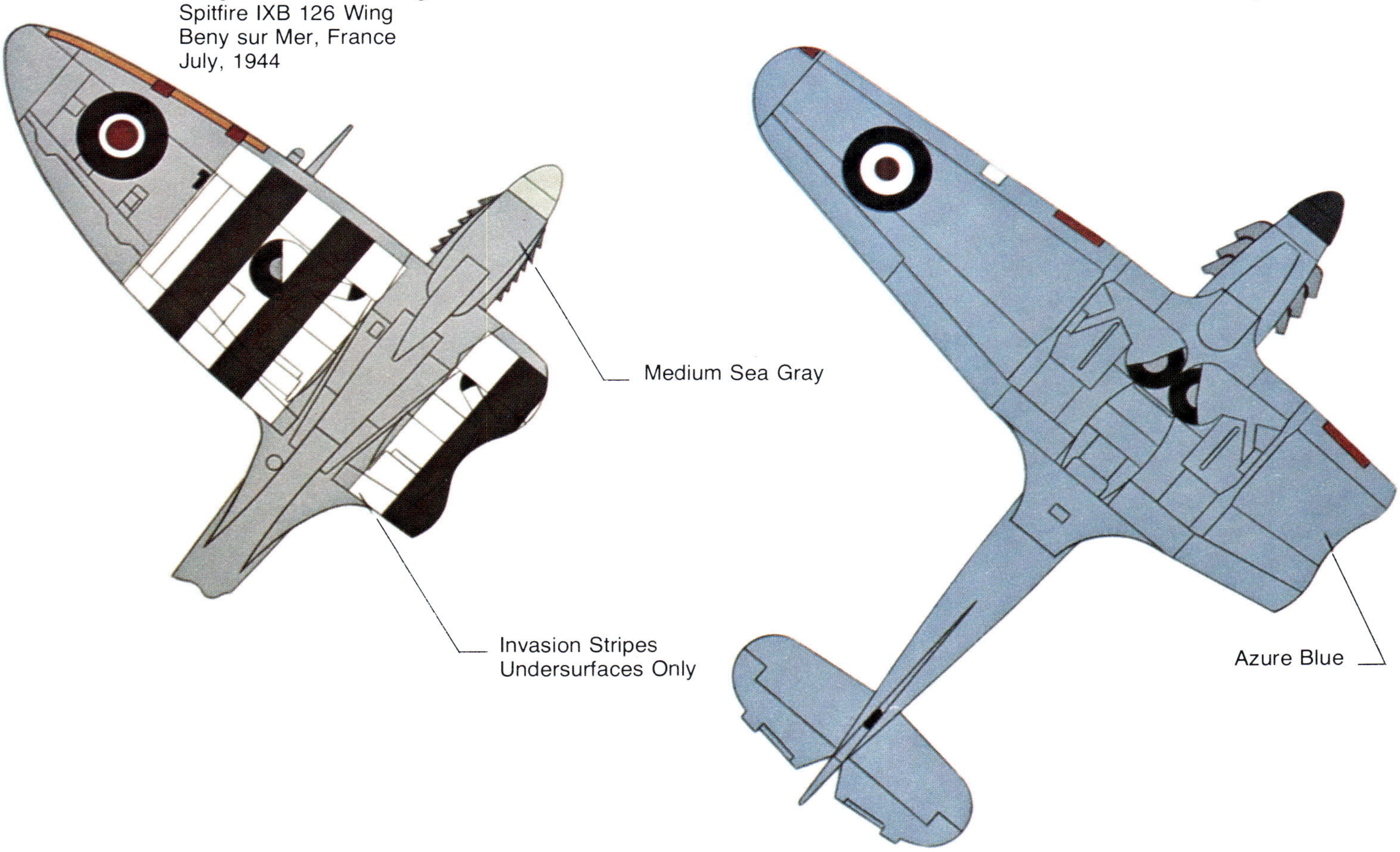

Wing Commander George Keefer
Hurricane IIB 274 Squadron
El Adem, Egypt April, 1942

Command Pennant on
Both Sides

Wing Commander Michael M. Stephens
Spitfire VB Takali, Malta
Spring, 1943

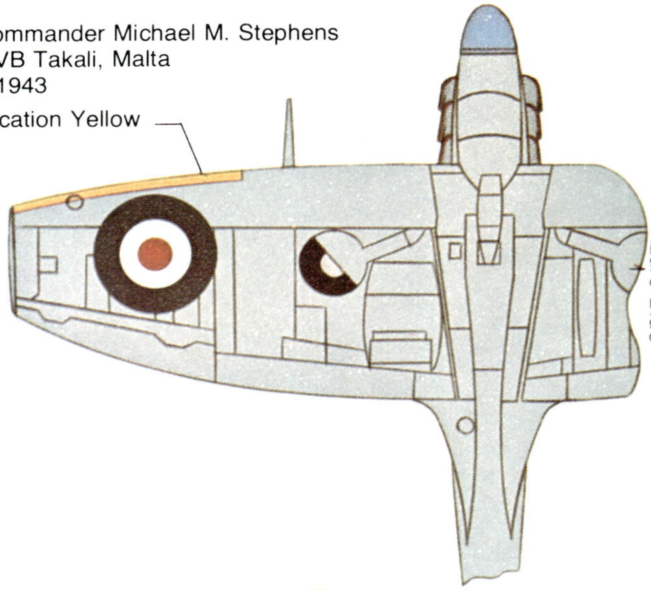

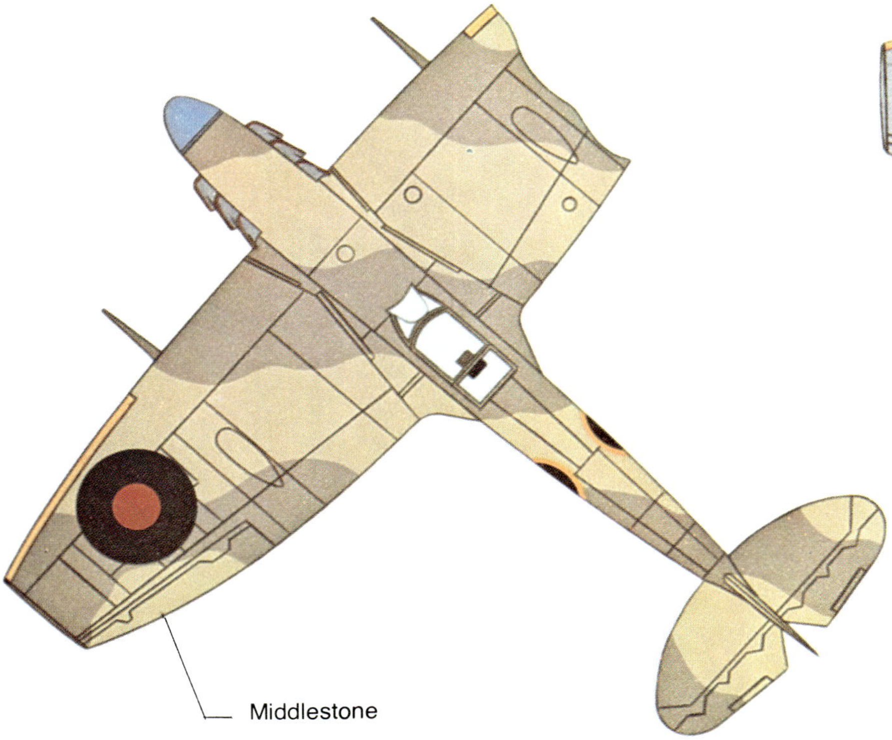

Wing Commander Robert McNair
Spitfire IXB 403 Squadron
Kenly, Middlesex, England
April, 1943

Victory and Fighter Sweep
Markings On Left Side Only

Colonel Eugene Roberts
P-47C 78th Fighter Group
Duxford, England Summer, 1943

Neutral Gray

Personal Markings
Both Sides

Inside Wheel Cover

Olive Drab

Command Pennant On
Both Sides

Overall Aircraft
Natural Metal

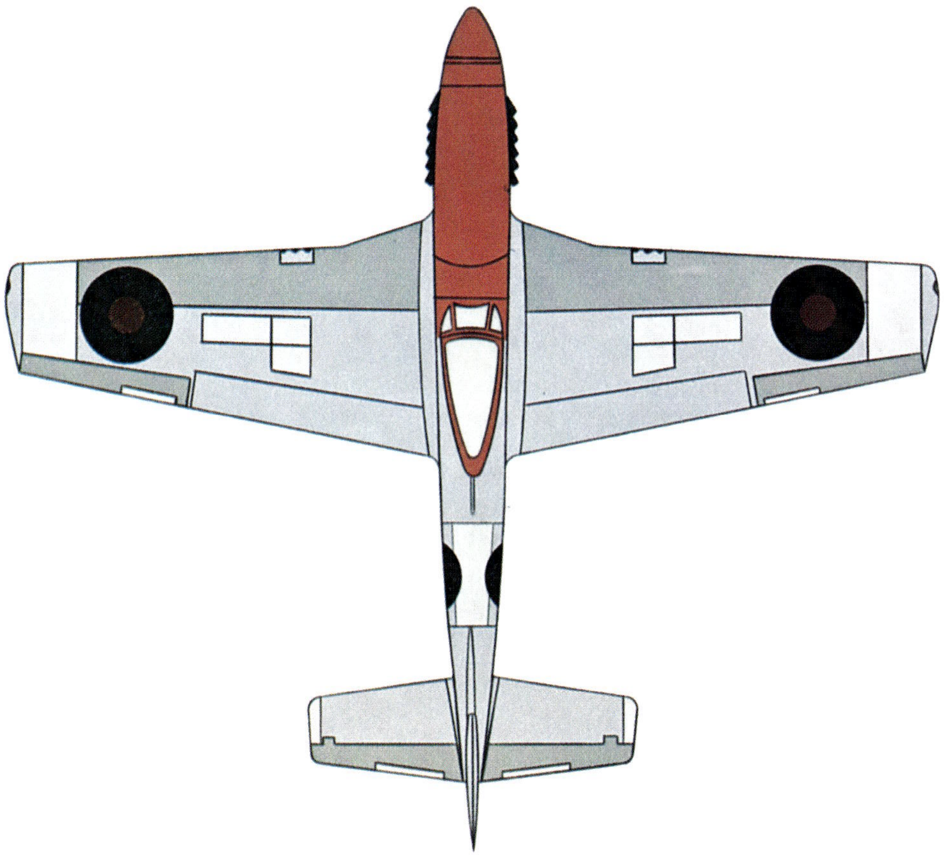

Wing Commander James Storrar
Mustang IV 239 Wing
Italy April, 1945

KAISER, Colonel Herbert
JG 77
Luftwaffe
(68 Victories)

Born on March 16, 1916 in Jessen on the Elster River in what is now East Germany, Herbert Kaiser attended the local grade school until he was fourteen at which time he became a journalistic apprentice for the next four years. When he reached eighteen, Kaiser became part of the German Labor Service, in which he served for two years. On April 1, 1936 just two weeks after his twentieth birthday, he entered an air force reserve unit. This was the beginning of an aviation career which spanned the length of World War II.

Colonel Herbert Kaiser who recently retired from the West German Air Force, was only one of 24 to pass the strenuous and exhaustive physical and written tests for acceptance to primary sea-flight instruction in 1936. At Puetnitz he was introduced to the Focke-Wulf Stoesser, the Heinkel He 51, and the Arado 68. Although the planes were slow, they were forgiving, and allowed the inexperienced pilot to profit by his mistakes, providing an excellent platform to indulge in stunt flying. Kaiser graduated with a certificate qualifying him for both land and sea based aircraft and was transferred to the Fighter School at Werneuchen, near Berlin, for advanced training and assignment. It was here that he was introduced to the plane he was to pilot for the next seven years, the Messerschmitt Me 109. It was not as cordial as the docile trainers, but he was to score 68 confirmed aerial victories with it.

As Colonel Kaiser describes it: **"The Me 109B was not an easy aircraft to fly. It had to be directed with utmost attention from the split-second one gave it gas. The extremely narrow tracked undercarriage could not fully compensate for the normal tendency of the aircraft to pull to the right due to the prop torque. The maintaining of one's starting direction could be accomplished only by the smooth application of power, the balancing of the rudder, and the balancing of the elevators to lift the tail only after airborne in order to keep constant aileron efficiency. Any casual disregard for these basic rules had a result of breaking the flight path and possible crash."**

"The cardinal rule during landing was that at the point of touchdown the gear and tail skid had to be oriented in the line of projected roll without further attempt at directional control. Separation of the aerodynamic lift due to insufficient approach speed, and excessive directional corrections performed during the landing procedure was the most common cause of crashes. The experienced pilot had these rules in his flesh and blood and this enabled him to make better use of his time by concentrating on other matters."

"Visibility from the cockpit was good, although during takeoff it was quite restricted in the frontal area until the tail wheel left the ground. It was not at all reassuring to look forward and see only the large metal cowl, and this was why the aircraft had to be correctly oriented on take off.

"Although the Me 109B was useful as a frontline combat aircraft and far outclassed enemy aircraft of the time in speed and climbing ability, its initial Junkers-built engine was extremely sensitive and not sufficiently powered."

"The Luftwaffe did not, in my estimation, have a truly superior and robust fighter aircraft until the appearance of the Me 109E. The use of the DB 601 engine with 1200 hp, the increased speed, and the high climb rate made the Me 109E, in relation to her counterparts, the best fighter of her time. Her armament of two machine guns and three cannon were more than enough to knock any enemy plane out of the air with a well placed burst of fire."

Under the leadership and instruction of Captain Hannes Trautloft (later General and Kommodore of JG 54 "Green Hearts"), Kaiser completed his training and on July 1, 1938 was posted to 2/132 (2nd **staffel** of Fighter Wing 132) in Jever under the command of Major Carl Schumacher. His **staffel** leader at this time was one Johannes Steinhoff who was to become one of the Luftwaffe's greatest leaders and who today is a General in the New German Air Force at NATO Headquarters in Brussels, Belgium.

In the fall of 1938, Kaiser's unit was assigned to support the occupation of the Sudentenland flying Me 109s. A struggle with the Czechs was expected, but much to his dismay, Kaiser found no aircraft rising to his challenge. Shortly after the occupation, Kaiser was posted to a carrier group in Keil-Holtenau, a large harbor on the Baltic Sea. This group was to be composed of a Me 109B fighter **staffel** and a Ju 87 Stuka dive bombing **staffel,** however, the initial training was carried out with specially equipped Heinkel He 50s. These slow speed training planes had arrestor hooks added to them in order to familiarize the pilots with the tactics of carrier landings and take-offs before they tried it with the faster, more tempermental, Me 109s. Take-offs and landings were conducted on a giant outlined landing surface in Travemuende which was rigged with arresting wires and recovery gear to simulate the deck of the German Navy's aircraft carrier **Graf Zeppelin,** then under construction.

When the decision was made by the German ministry not to build the **Graf Zeppelin,** Kaiser and his fighter **staffel** were transferred to East Prussia for the upcoming invasion of Poland. On September 1, 1939 at 6:00 p.m. they took to the air for their first real combat mission. Their orders were to provide cover escort for the advanced Stuka flights whose target was the Polish Navy's anchorage at Hela in the Bay of Danzig. Although flak was heavy from the Polish anti-aircraft batteries surrounding the harbor, no aerial opposition was encountered due mostly to the surprise of the attack.

On September 20, 1939 Kaiser's unit was pulled back and transferred to Cuxhaven, in Germany. From here he flew continuous patrol duty and cover flights over the Heligoland Bight (German Bay) now mounted in the Me 109E. On May 6th Kaiser achieved his first victory while carrying out an interception mission with his wingman. Vectored to intercept two Royal Air Force Bristol Blenheims approaching the coast, the **rotte** sighted the Blenheims, but were in turn spotted by the RAF bombers who quickly turned toward home, wanting no part of an engagement with the approaching 109s. Giving chase, Kaiser and his wingman caught the Blenheims near the Isle of Tershchelling and destroyed them. The next day he was decorated with the German Iron Cross 2nd Class.

On May 10, 1940 Kaiser, now flying as part of III/JG 77 took part in the start of the Western Campaign against airfields in Holland and was credited with the destruction of two Dutch Fokker D 21s. He was then sent to France where he remained, flying patrol until the Dunkirk encirclement.

Of these days Kaiser relates: **"Although prior to the start of the Western Campaign in May 1940, no German pilot could make a comprehensive comparison between British and French fighters and our Me 109E, we firmly believed we had the best airplane based on comparative flying reports and an abundance of rumors. Personally, at the advent of hostilities, I had contact only with Dutch Fokker D 21s, and this fixed geared monoplane, approximately 50 mph slower than a 109E, offered no particular challenge. Some of my comrades from neighboring units, however, had encountered the RAF Spitfires and Hurricanes, as well as the French Dewoitines and Morane Saulniers and affirmed what we all had believed about our aircraft."**

"In personally facing the RAF in the air over the Dunkirk encirclement, I found that the Me 109E was faster, possessed a higher rate of climb, but was somewhat less maneuverable than the RAF fighters. Nevertheless, during the campaign, no Spitfire or Hurricane ever turned inside of my plane, and after the war the RAF admitted the loss of 450 Hurricanes during the Battle of France.

One June 19, 1941 III/JG 77 was posted to Bacau on the Russian border and on the 21st engaged in their first missions against the Russian Air Force. Taking off at 4:00 a.m. Kaiser achieved his initial kill over the Eastern Front later in the day near Balti.

Colonel Kaiser recalls the Russian campaign: **"Against the early Russian aircraft the Me 109E was untouchable. The Soviet planes were slower and could**

First Me 109 in the Western Desert was the E model, this one from I/JG 27. Mottle dark brown over sand was typical of early camouflage schemes.

not climb with us. They were, however, highly maneuverable, especially the I-15 and I-16, and one could not allow an encounter to deteriorate into a contest of turns. This was easily avoided, because we always had the element of surprise, due to our high speed and advanced communication systems."

"In Russia I encountered many varied aircraft, particularly bombers, for the most part the twin engined Ilyushin DB-3, and later the Pe-2, and IL-2 attack bombers. The greatest losses for the Soviets, at least in our sector, occurred with the DB-3. A military version of a Soviet long distance record-breaker, it had great range, but was incredibly slow, and possessed poor defensive firepower. All weapons were hand-held, rifle-caliber guns and the bomber was blind to a direct tail on approach. A single burst between the left engine and the fuselage into the wing root and the unprotected fuel tanks, guaranteed immediate burning and unavoidable crash. It was considerably more difficult to attack the Pe-2 because of her speed, twin-tail assembly and the unrestricted tail gunner's vision."

The Ilyushin IL-2—Stormovik—was also tough. A single engine fighter bomber, not exceptionally fast, but very well armored, this plane required a detailed knowledge of its construction and a well executed approach to destroy. The unforgettable Moelders showed me personally how one downed this aircraft. The IL-2 possessed head armour behind the pilot; but just behind this armour was a small tank which was utilized as a starter cartridge. Totally unprotected and vulnerable, this tank was exploded with a single incendiary burst. Of course, in this mode of attack, a precise and accurate burst was necessary. Later the Soviets installed a rear gunner's position and armored the starter cartridge."

"During my participation in the Russian campaign, I also encountered the Lagg 3 and the Mig 3. I did destroy some of these, but it would be extremely difficult to make any well founded comparison with the Me 109 because of my limited confrontation."

Following the thrust of the German Army, Kaiser and III/JG 77 arrived in the Crimea where they continued their duel with the Soviet air forces. They were now flying Me 109Fs. During the crossing of the Dnieper River, upon returning from a recon flight over the area, Kaiser sighted a group of 27 Martin Maryland bombers (lend-lease aircraft) and destroyed three of them, attacking the formation from below and behind.

From the Crimea, Kaiser flew over Sebastopol in December 1941 and over Kursk in January 1942, his first winter campaign. Despite the freezing Russian winter, by June he had raised his victory total to 46, at which time he was transferred north for the second push on Moscow. The second summer of war in Russia resulted in stalemate and with the arrival of an early winter, Kaiser and III/JG 77 were again transferred, this time to Africa, arriving at Tobruk on October 20th.

It was in North Africa that Kaiser received his first Me 109G; "Here I was introduced to the Me 109G which had an even more powerful engine than the F model and a larger compressor (supercharger). It also had extremely good high altitude performance. The air density of the North African sky was considerably less than that over Russia, and our performance could be maintained only through the constant use of the compressor. From a pure flying standpoint, the Me 109G offered little over the Me 109F. She was considerably heavier and still had the difficult take off and landing qualities inherent with all the Me 109 variants."

"During the African campaign, we were short of aircraft and for the young pilots with little actual air or combat experience, it was very difficult to master the 109. In addition, landings and takeoffs were aggravated by the general condition of the desert air strips, not to mention sand and blowing grit. Because of these conditions, the relatively few number of flight worthy planes were usually flown by the older, more experienced pilots, and the appearance of the same familiar names dominated the victory totals."

From Tobruk, the unit moved back to El Alamein, but Kaiser requested to stay behind for an extra day in order to visit an old friend before leaving. When Kaiser finally took off in company with his wingman, who also had remained he encountered a group of six Curtiss P-40s strafing the Tobruk supply routes. He recalls this action very vividly; "I had flown about a half a mile when I sighted the enemy formation of P-40s strafing a convoy on the main German supply route into Tobruk. I would not have even noticed the RAF formation if it had not been for the geysers of dirt and sand their shells were kicking up around the convoy. At first glance I still could not make out how many of the enemy there were, due to the blending of the camouflage with the desert setting below. Finally I was able to identify the P-40s making single file strafing runs and turned to the attack. They were so intent on their work they failed to notice me. I dove on the last aircraft from above and behind letting him have a short burst. As my shells ripped into his aircraft and he went down, the pilot must have managed to radio the rest of the flight, for they immediately made a steep left turn and headed out into the desert in a zig-zagging pattern, their formation appearing like a snake on the desert floor. Within about 40 miles, I caught up with them and again pressed home an attack which resulted in the destruction of a second P-40. In the heat of the battle, however, I became reckless and as I watched the second P-40 crash into the sand I noticed flashes across my wing. Another of the RAF aircraft had gotten on my tail and was pouring fire into my fuselage and wings, disabling my oil and water systems. I pulled my Me 109G into a steep turn and looked for a place to put my aircraft down as I was too low to bail out. As my plane skidded across the sand, the dust was so thick I couldn't tell if I was on fire or not. Fortunately, for me, the aircraft did not burn."

Kaiser's wingman, who was also engaged in aerial combat, mistook the flying dust for smoke and upon landing at the unit's new base in El Alamein, reported the death of his commander. Kaiser, however, after a four hour hike across the sand, reached the main Tobruk supply road, where he was picked up by German forces and returned to his base at El Alamein much to the surprise of his comrades.

Between October 28th and November 5th, he accounted for four more enemy planes, but was himself wounded and sent to Athens for two weeks to recover. He rejoined the group on November 21, 1942 in Bengahzi and on his return to flying status quickly shot down a Spitfire V.

Describing the tactics employed by the Luftwaffe in North Africa in late 1942 and his impressions of some of the air-

The last 109 to see action in Africa was the G model. Even with additional 70 gallon drop tank, fighter was range poor, a characteristic of both British and German interceptors designed before the war.

craft he faced, Colonel Kaiser relates; **"The classic dogfight was still partly used in Africa, and the lone sortie was prevalent. We were forced to this lone sortie tactic of surprise due to the overwhelming supply of Allied aircraft and, in this way, were able to spread ourselves over more area. Any other tactics would be coupled with high losses on our side, a condition we could not allow. Additionally, the speed and durability of the Me 109G lent itself very well to this type of tactic. If we were overmatched, we could always break off."**

"The Curtiss P-40 was not as fast as the Me 109G and in a confrontation with this plane we had nothing to worry about as long as the basic rules of combat tactics were followed. We did, however, have to avoid getting into the middle of a large formation, for the P-40 turned well and, as an old German saying goes "Too many dogs are the death of the rabbit."

"The P-38 Lightning was equal to our Me 109G in performance, far superior in range, and was a much more difficult adversary in a dogfight. However, I never employed any special evasive maneuvers when I encountered one of them. Evasive tactics, as far as I am concerned, were dictated by the situation and were a reflex reaction. For the most part, independent of the aircraft on your tail, one would utilize a steep turn and pull out to get behind his enemy, or pull up on the stick in a succession of stuttering steps to reduce speed, hoping the abrupt velocity decrease would not be picked up in time by the aircraft behind you, forcing him to fly by exposing his belly. I always considered a turn out and dive a high risk tactic and, to my knowledge, this particular move was not used to any great extent by Luftwaffe fighter pilots."

In January 1943, Kaiser was detached from JG 77 and sent to a replacement depot in Southern France as an instructor. He stayed here for four months before rejoining III/JG 77 on the Island of Sardinia. He was then transferred within the wing to I/JG 77 and posted to Italy where he destroyed four more aircraft. Then in January 1944, Kaiser was returned to Germany for a routine medical checkup after which he was assigned to I/JG 1 under the command of Colonel Walter Oesau. With this unit he flew until June 6, 1944 in the Defense of the Reich. From June 6th until August 9th he was stationed on the Normandy Front flying in a defensive role against the Allied invasion forces and describes his experiences as follows:

"Near the end of June 1944 while attached to I/JG 1, on an airfield just outside Paris, France, an excellent example of the almost complete Allied air superiority occurred. I was vectored out to intercept an incoming flight of Allied bombers which was attacking our troops in the Normandy area. Our take-off had to be only in the smallest of flights (usually 2 to 4 aircraft) due to the Allied fighters which almost always waited above the bases for our fighters to emerge from cloud cover. We would be forced to sneak from our base into our target area by hedge hopping over the terrain to take advantage of all the camouflage possible. Flying only a few feet off the ground kept us off radar screens, but sometimes put us on the side of a hill. We would only climb to heights when we reached the attack point under the enemy planes."

"My flight of four aircraft sighted a formation of escorting Spitfires, and we positioned ourselves to engage them. We were instead caught by a second group of Allied fighters and in the process I lost my three men. Escape from the onslaught seemed impossible. Only because of my experience and the lucky appearance of a nearby cloud was I able to save myself."

"At this time the Luftwaffe was being ground into the earth. One could not count on his hand the days he expected to live. It was surprising to me that the Luftwaffe pilot had any nerve left at all, let alone the ability to prepare himself for combat with the enemy under these conditions."

On August 9th Kaiser himself was shot down and badly wounded. On this day his **staffel** was vectored to intercept a formation of approximately 300 Allied aircraft. In preparing for the attack on the RAF Lancaster bombers in the Allied flight, he was jumped from the sun and hit by a Spitfire. He hurriedly opened the canopy of his burning Me 109G and bailed out only to entangle his right leg in his parachute shroud. Badly wounded and with a multiple fracture of his right thigh, he landed behind German lines and remained in a hospital inside Germany until February 1945 at which time he joined Adolf Galland's famous JV 44 flying the Me 262 jet from Munich-Reim. Unable to control the new aircraft due to his still sensitive leg injuries, Kaiser remained with the unit and directed the wing's aircraft to enemy formations from the ground control center.

On May 7th the unit surrendered at Salzburg to advancing American forces, but Kaiser and a fellow pilot escaped and made their way back to Munich on foot where he reached a discharge station and was mustered out of the Luftwaffe. On July 30th he reached his home town of Jessen.

Colonel Kaiser sums up his wartime career by saying: **"In all, I flew over 1,400 combat sorties over enemy territory. While in Poland and during the early Western Campaign these missions were limted. However, after 1941 the number of missions per day increased to two and sometimes three a day depending on the particular situation that we faced, and of course, on the weather. In late 1944 and into early 1945 every one of our pilots on active combat duty, veteran or not, was flying three to four missions every single day for as long as his body and mind could take these exhaustive conditions. Some flew even more."**

"Except for my time in Africa where supply lines were long and the conditions abnormal, I can not complain about the shortage of replacement parts or the technical maintenance our aircraft received. I always had a very high respect and trust for my ground crew and cannot remember ever having a problem with their ability or dedication to both myself and our Me 109. The supply of new planes, however, was not at all times what I would consider comfortable. It usually just kept up with the demand."

Best dogfighting 109 was the F model, this one shot down during the battle of El Alamein, in November, 1942, was from III/JG 27's third squadron. Large fitting on air intake is a desert filter.

Kaiser's aircraft appears on page 41.

KASHIIDE, Captain Isamu
4th Fighter Sentai
Imperial Japanese Army Air Force
(33 Victories)

Isamu Kashiide, born in Kashizaki City in Niigata Prefecture on November 2, 1915, attended local schools there until February 1, 1934 at which time he was admitted to the Japanese Army Aviation School in Tokorozawa as a flying student first class. He graduated with honors on November 25, 1935 and four days later entered the Akeno Flying School for fighter pilot instruction. Assigned to the 1st Air Force Regiment in Gifu, Japan, he remained attached to this unit for almost two and a half years until July 1938 at which time he was posted to the 59th Fighter Sentai where, in August he participated in the Russian-Manchurian Border clashes, flying a Ki.10 "Perry". On August 25th the unit was transferred to the central China area for the support of Japanese forces engaging the Chinese. A year later he was back fighting in the Russian-Manchurian Border War, flying from a base inside Manchuria. Two months later, on October 11th, a cease fire was called, and Kashiide, who had been credited with six enemy aircraft, returned to Central China to an air base at Kankow.

On March 1, 1940 Kashiide was transferred to the 4th Sentai in Tachiarai, Japan as a flight instructor where he taught for nine months before he was sent to the Army Air Force Academy for officer's training and advanced fighter tactics. On October 1, 1941 he graduated and was promoted to the rank of second lieutenant. On December 8, 1941, Kashiide as part of the 4th Fighter Sentai, attacked United States bases in the Philippines from forward air strips on Taiwan. After the fail of the Philippines, the 4th Sentai was sent to Kumamoto, Japan for rest and needed repair to damaged aircraft. From here they were sent to Kozuki, Yamaguchi-ken, Japan on the western tip of Honshu. As with most Japanese Army Air Force units based on the home islands the 4th was assigned the duty of protecting Japan from reprisal attacks from Allied bombers. Expecting any raid to come from bases inside China, the assignment was very uneventful until the Doolittle Raid on April 18, 1942. Taken completely by surprise by the low-flying B-25 medium bombers which had been launched from the carrier deck of the USS *Hornet*, Japan's loosely organized Air Defense Command now took on a new importance, and the 4th Sentai became a vital part of it. Flying obsolete Nakajima Ki. 27 Nates, the unit began intensive training on interception tactics and procedures against both high altitude and low flying bomber formations. From their base at Kozuki, the 4th was given the responsibility of providing air protection for the area from Yawata to Kokura Island which contained a heavy concentration of the Japanese war industry.

During their training and tactics instruction, the 4th *Sentai* began to realize that as the size, range and firepower of the American bombers increased, the effectiveness of their already obsolete Ki. 27's was almost nil. The unit was therefore re-equipped with the heavy twin-engine attack fighter, the Kawasaki Ki. 45 Toryu (Nick) in early 1943. In addition to the new plane, night flying instruction was also introduced and Kashiide, along with other members of the unit, were sent to Navigational School in Manchuria in November of 1943.

Kashiide's first combat with the Boeing B-29 Superfortress occurred on June 1944 when his *Chutai* was ordered to intercept a formation of incoming Allied bombers. Taking off in the dark of night, the group was vectored to a point of contact over the Upper Onga River area. Kashiide sighted the enemy planes at approximately 12,000 feet over Wakamatsu and immediately dove toward the bombers for an attack. At a distance of only 250 feet from the third bomber in the formation, Kashiide fired

Kashide's Ki. 45 Nick was formidable, well armed and included one nose mounted 37mm cannon and two obliquely-mounted 20mm weapons behind cockpit. Japanese pilots maneuvered their heavy Kawasaki fighters below B-29's belly and fired upward into that rather large and relatively unprotected area.

his 37mm cannon and saw its shells impact between the left wing and fuselage of the B-29. Barely missing the burning bomber, Kashiide dove beneath it and then climbed up again to watch the plane spin into the river below. The time was now 3:00 a.m. June 17th.

After the attack, the first by the new B-29 Superfortress, night training became even more intense for Kashiide and his unit. Each time the B-29 formations flew over, they changed their flight patterns and spacing, attempting to ready themselves to react to any circumstance. Kashiide, as Commander of the 3rd *Chutai*, 4th *Sentai*, instructed his pilots to attack from behind and slightly below the bomber formations, if possible, as this was the area of minimum enemy gun protection.

On March 27, 1945 sixty B-29s attacked the Yawata steel making complex and the 4th again took off to intercept and destroy the formations. During this action, Kashiide enjoyed his best day against the big "Superforts" and was credited with destroying three of them while damaging three others.

On August 6th, a flight of four B-29s from an Allied base in Korea neared a small island of Takeshima which was under the defense umbrella assigned to the 4th *Sentai*. Flying at an altitude of approximately 21,000 feet they appeared to be faster to Kashiide than the previous Superfortresses he had engaged. As Kashiide's *Chutai* approached the point of interception over Hiroshima, he noticed the large unfamiliar mushroom cloud of smoke and immediately reported the bombardment.

Not knowing that he had just witnessed the dropping of the first atomic bomb, Kashiide could not comprehend the enormous damage he was seeing. All around him the white smoke billowed upward with a huge black center. All this damage, and by only four planes.

A few days later, Kashiide again was scrambled to intercept a formation of B-29s, this time over Nagasaki. As he had done at Hiroshima, he again was witness to the most devastating destruction ever seen by man.

On August 15th, the Emperor of Japan announced the war's end, and Kashiide, though shaken, could not help but reflect on his survival. Out of the seventy pilots who had graduated with him, twenty-eight had flown under him in the 4th *Sentai*. When the war ended only three were still alive. Kashiide had been credited with the destruction of 33 enemy planes including six I-15s and I-16s during the Russian-Manchurian Border War and twenty-six B-29 Superfortresses. His twenty-six B-29s was the highest score achieved by any Japanese pilot against these aircraft. He was also decorated with several medals for his actions, including the Distinguished Medal for Bravery, one of Japan's highest awards, for his three victories on March 27, 1945. Even more spectacular, however, was his presence at the two most awesome and controversial air attacks in the history of aerial warfare.

The Ki.45 Toryu piloted by Kashiide as commander of the 3rd Chutai, 4th Fighter Sentai at Kozuki, Japan in March 1945 is illustrated on page 37.

Captured by U.S. Technical Intelligence Unit and subsequently evaluated, Kawasaki Ki. 45 proved very maneuverable and had a top speed of 340 mph., a cruise of 236 mph. and a range of 930 miles.

Ki. 45 flown by Captain Kashide at Kozuki, Japan, March 1945. Kashide shot down three B-29s in this aircraft and witnessed the destruction of Nagasaki and Hiroshima, by A-bombs, from its cockpit.

KEARBY, Colonel Neel
342nd Fighter Squadron
348th Fighter Group
5th Air Force
(22 Victories)

Born on June 5, 1911 in Wichita Falls, Texas, Neel Earnest Kearby enlisted in the United States Army Air Forces on February 25, 1937 at March Field, California. As a Flying Cadet, he received his primary training at Randolph Field, Texas and in October was sent to Advanced Flying School at Kelly Field, where he completed training in February 1938. He was commissioned as a Second Lieutenant, Air Corps Reserve with the rating of pilot and was immediately called to extended active duty with the Air Corps and assigned to the 94th Pursuit Squadron, 1st Pursuit Group, General Headquarters Air Force, Selfridge Field, Michigan.

In June Kearby was transferred to the 14th Pursuit Squadron, 53rd Pursuit Group as a Squadron Commander at Tallahassee, Florida. Shortly after the attack on Pearl Harbor, Kearby was reassigned to Howard Field, Panama Canal Zone, and later to Westover Field, Massachusetts, finally being shipped overseas as part of the 348th on May 15, 1943 for duty in the Asiatic-Pacific Theater.

The 348th entered combat for the first time in the early summer under Kearby's command. Promoted to the rank of Lt. Colonel on August 23rd, he was in charge of the 5th Air Force's only P-47 Thunderbolt unit. On October 11, 1943 Kearby volunteered to lead a flight of four fighters to reconnoiter the strongly defended enemy base at Wewak. After having mapped Japanese installations and reinforcements at four separate airfields, he sighted a Japanese Zero below him and dove in to attack. The enemy plane burst into flames and plummeted to the earth below. Kearby then sighted a formation of approximately twelve Japanese bombers and thirty-six escorting fighters. Although his flight had completed its assigned duty, and not considering the fact that their fuel was low and they were outnumbered by twelve to one, Kearby gave the order to attack. Diving into the center of the enemy formation, Kearby destroyed three of the enemy aircraft in quick succession, then, observing one of his pilots with two Japanese Ki 61s on his tail, he broke off an attack he was conducting and in the following melee downed both of the pursuers. The Japanese formation broke off in large numbers to make a multiple attack on Kearby's P-47, but despite his peril, he made one more pass before seeking cloud cover protection. After coming into the clear Kearby assembled his flight and led them back to Port Moresby, New Guinea. During this action Kearby was credited with six confirmed victories and for his daring leadership was decorated with the Congressional Medal of Honor.

On November 12, 1943, Kearby was relieved of his command with the 348th Fighter Group and was transferred to the Headquarters Squadron, V Fighter Command. He remained there until February 1944 when he was posted to Headquarters Squadron, 308th Bombardment Wing. On February 26th he was appointed Commanding Officer of the 309th Bombardment Wing.

On March 4, 1944, Kearby took off with his Headquarters flight of four aircraft headed for the Wewak area. Just west of the Japanese airfield at Dagua, the flight sighted a formation of approximately fifteen enemy fighters and Kearby signaled for an attack. On the first pass he destroyed one of the enemy, and turning back into the formation, flamed a second to run his total score to twenty-two. As he was pulling out of his second run, he was set upon by three of the enemy aircraft and was, himself, shot down and killed.

Kearby was decorated with the Silver Star with One Oak Leaf Cluster, the Distinguished Flying Cross with three Oak Leaf Clusters, the Air Medal with four Oak Leaf Clusters, and the Congressional Medal of Honor. Four months after his death, Kearby was posthumously awarded the permanent rank of Colonel in the Army Air Forces, the temporary rank he held from September 23, 1943 until his death.

KEEFER, Wing Commander George C.
126 Wing
Royal Canadian Air Force
(12 Victories)

Keefer, standing, and Lt. John Lane, after he rescued the latter from the desert near Bir Hacheim.

George Clinton Keefer was born on July 11, 1921 in New York City, New York. His mother was Canadian, his father an American. He completed high school at Phillips Exeter Academy in New Hampshire before enrolling at Yale University to study engineering. One year later, in October 1940, he enlisted in the Royal Canadian Air Force and was sent to the Manning Depot at Toronto and in December was assigned to No. 1 Initial Flying School in Toronto. In December Keefer was sent on to the Elementary Flying School at Cap de la Madeleine, Quebec, where he flew in Fleet Finches both on wheels and on skis. He soloed after only four hours of dual flying and completed thirty-four total hours of air time before he was graduated and sent to No. 2 Service Flying Training School at Uplands, Ontario, where he piloted North American Harvards (AT-6s) and Yales. Keefer graduated in April 1941 and was commissioned as a Pilot Officer on April 11th when he received orders to ship overseas to England.

Keefer arrived in England on June 6, 1941 and was posted to No. 59 Operational Training Unit at Crosby-on-Eden where he was introduced to the Hawker Hurricane. Between June and August he collected over 200 hours in the Hurricane before being assigned combat duty with 274 Squadron in Egypt. Keefer picked up his Hurricane II from the maintenance depot and ferried it to Abbotsinch-on-the-Clyde for loading on board the HMS *Furious*. At Gibraltar, the aircraft were transferred to HMS *Ark Royal* where they remained until they were within easy range of Malta. The Hurricanes then flew first to Malta and from there on to Egypt where they landed at Faiyum near Cairo. Keefer joined 274 Squadron at Lake Maryut just outside Alexandria. The unit was in the air continuously, performing anti-shipping type patrols, from here as well as Port Said, until the unit moved to Sidi Henish in the desert where they were re-equipped with Hurricane IIs to replace their Hurricane Is and Tomahawks. From here the unit initiated operational fighter sweeps, strafing missions, and interception flights against the Luftwaffe. On December 7, 1941, Keefer had his first encounter with the enemy when the unit was vectored to intercept a formation of Luftwaffe Ju 87s, Me 109s and Italian Macchi 200s. During the aerial encounter Keefer was credited with his first victory when he destroyed one of the escorting Macchi 200s. For the next few months the unit moved continually from one base to another avoiding the German Forces. From Sidi Henish they moved to Msus, Michili, Gazala, and finally El Adem. During this time Keefer took part in almost continuous air combat with the German and Italian Air Forces. Finally on April 7th, the unit was pulled out of front line duty back to Sidi Henish for re-equipping and rest, but on May 7th, 274 Squadron moved back up to Gambut and the fighting started again.

On June 4, 1942 the town of Bir Hacheim was being held by the Free French ground forces. The city had been surrounded and by-passed by the Germans. 274 Squadron was assigned patrol duty to this area and as the flight approached the city they encountered a formation of 109s. After an inconclusive air battle, Keefer sighted someone on the desert floor approximately 10 miles northeast of Bir Hacheim waving a "Mae West". He decided to land and investigate, and found Lt. John Lane from No. 4 Squadron of the South African Air Force who had been shot down in an earlier engagement. Keefer picked him up and the two pilots flew back to Gambut. Four days later, on June 8th, Keefer was in the ready room with A Flight preparing for a bombing mission, again over Bir Hacheim. Taking off with B Flight as cover, Keefer dropped his bomb load and was in the process of reforming when he sighted a Macchi 202 below him. Keefer dove to the attack and opened up just over the desert surface. The enemy rolled over as flames blossomed from the fuselage and went straight into the sand below.

Keefer stayed with 274 Squadron until August 25th at which time he had accounted for four enemy aircraft and had logged over 200 hours and 179 combat missions. He was posted to Air Fighting School at No. 1 Middle East Training School at El Baccah and remained here as an instructor for over six months before he was finally posted back to combat duty with 402 Squadron (RCAF) flying Spitfire Vbs at Digby, England on April 10, 1943. Keefer stayed with 402 for only a month before he was transferred to 416 Squadron (RCAF) flying Spitfire IXs from Kenly. After a few sorties over France and a few aerial encounters with the Luftwaffe over the Channel, Keefer again was reassigned, this time to 412 Squadron at Perranporth in Cornwall as a Flight Commander. For the rest of May and the early part of June Keefer took part in convoy patrol over the Channel, bomber escort missions over France, and an occasional fighter sweep against German troops on the occupied mainland. By the end of June Keefer had been promoted to the rank of Squadron Leader and was given command of the unit. On July 27th, Keefer experienced his first real close call when his Spitfire was hit by enemy fire near Abbeville and sprang a glycol leak. After a short time the engine froze up and he barely made it to the French coast. Keefer bailed out over the Channel and was picked up four hours later by a RAF Air/Sea Rescue Walrus and flown back to Hawkinge. On August 6th the Squadron moved to 126 Airfield at Staplehurst and began training for support of the coming invasion of the continent. Re-equipped with Spitfire IXBs at Biggin Hill in November, 412 Squadron combined their training program with sweeps over the French countryside and occasional encounters with the Luftwaffe.

In April 1944 Keefer was promoted to the rank of Wing Commander and

Keefer's Spitfire IXB at Beny sur Mer, France, shortly after the Normandy invasion.

Early Mk. IX Spitfire with four .30 caliber machine guns and two 20mm cannon.

assumed command of 126 Wing (RCAF) at Biggin Hill which included 401, 411, and 412 Squadrons and on June 6, 1944, the day of the invasion of Normandy, he led his wing on four separate sorties over the beach area, but did not encounter any enemy opposition. The following day he returned to the beachhead and was credited with a Ju 88 to reach ace status. On June 10th the unit made their first operational flight from a beachhead airfield (B-3, two miles east of Crepon). On the 18th Keefer moved his unit to the main airfield at Beny-sur-mer and a week later was credited with a Me 110 and a Me 109. Keefer completed his tour of duty with 126 Wing on July 9th at which time he was relieved and returned to Canada for leave. Over the one month time period from June 6th to July 9th, 126 Wing, under his command, accounted for 56 enemy aircraft destroyed and 26 damaged in the air and had recorded the destruction or damage of 396 enemy ground transport vehicles.

Keefer returned to duty on November 12, 1944 as commander of 125 Wing (RAF) located at Diest, Belgium. The Wing included 41, 130, 350, and 402 Squadrons and was equipped with the only Spitfire XIVs stationed on the continent. Over the next few months Keefer's Wing took part in fighter action over "The Bulge" area and several ground strafing support sorties. Flying from an advance base (Y-32 just north of "The Bulge") on January 23, 1945, Keefer suffered another close call. His Spitfire was hit by the shrapnel from an exploding transport convoy he had just attacked and his engine quit. Keefer gained as much height as possible without power and then glided just far enough to crash land in front of the American lines. The following day the Wing moved to Eindhoven and from here Keefer led the Wing on escort and sweep missions into the heart of Germany. On March 2nd he was credited with the destruction of a Me 109 over the Rheine Airdrome and two weeks later was credited with another Me 109 in the same area. Following is the combat report from that mission.

● ● ● ● ● ● ● ● ● ●

SECRET

PERSONAL COMBAT REPORT REF: OPFLASH 125/19/1

Date: March 19th, 1945.
Squadron: W/Cdr Keefer (flying with 130 Punjab Squadron)
Type and Mark of Aircraft: Spitfire XIV.
Time Up and Down: 0855-1015
Time of Attack: 0930.
Place of Attack: Rheine Aerodrome.
Height of enemy at first sighting: Deck level to 2,000 ft.
Own height on first sighting: 12,000 ft.
Was cine-camera used: Yes.
Was gyro sight used: Yes.
Enemy casualties: One Me 109 destroyed by W/Cdr G. Keefer D.C.O. D.F.C.

W/Cdr Keefer states:

I was leading 130 (Punjab) Squadron on a sweep in the Rheine-Osnabruck area and at about 0930 when we were at 12,000 ft between the aerodromes at Rheine and Hopsten e/a were reported below. I led the Squadron down and a dog fight began at deck level near Rheine aerodrome from which there was intense light flak. I found two Me 109s going round together in a tight turn. Eventually one straightened out and flew due east. I gave him a quick squirt from dead astern and saw strikes on the starboard wing. Closing in further I fired again and this time there were strikes on the top of the cockpit and I saw that the hood was dragging. The e/a slowed, pulled up and he stalled in from about 20 ft. I saw the e/a crash into a field. I claim this enemy aircraft destroyed.

W/O Miller who was Red 4 states that he saw the W/Cdr attacking this machine and that as he passed over it he saw that the tail assembly was badly damaged. Glycol was also pouring from the e/a.

Pilot making claim: Signed: "GC Keefer W/C"
Intelligence Officer: Signed: "R.M. Williams F/O"

On April 6th the Wing moved to Twente/Enschede and the following two weeks proved very lucrative for Keefer and his unit as is seen by the following combat reports filed by Keefer.

SECRET

PERSONAL COMBAT REPORT OPFLASH: 125/20/17

Date: 20 April, 1945
Sqn: 130 (Punjab) Sqdn.
Type and Mark of A/C: Spit XIV
Time Up and Down: 1913-2043
Time of Attack: 1940
Place of Attack: Wittstock
Height of Enemy on First Sighting: 6000'
Own Height on First Sighting: 5000'
Was cine gun used: Yes.
Was Gyro Sight Used: Yes.
Our Casualties: Nil.
Enemy Casulties: 1 F.W. 190 destroyed by W/Cmdr KEEFER, DSO, DFC

W/Cmdr Keefer states:

I was flying with 130 Sqn. and was leading Red Section. Our mission was an Armed Recce. About 1930 hrs. we were in the WITTSTOCK area at 5000' going N.E. when we spotted two M.E. 109s slightly above at 12 o'clock to us and going the same way. We opened up and caught up with the e/a. I picked one and opened fire at dead astern. I saw strikes on the fuselage. I gave him another burst at closer range whereupon the e/a caught fire, crashed into a field and exploded.

I claim this E/A Destroyed.

Signature of Pilot SIGNED: G. Keefer.
Signature of Intelligence Officer SIGNED: R.M. Williams, P/O

F/Lt Samuelle confirms this claim. He says, "I saw the W/Cmdr's combat and I saw the E/A hit the ground and blow up."

SIGNED: C.J. Samuelle, F/Lt.

SECRET

PERSONAL COMBAT REPORT REF: OPFLASH 125/25/1

Date: 25 Apr 45
Sqn: W. Cmdr. Keefer flying with 350 Sqn.
Type and Mark of Aircraft: Spitfire XIV
Time up and down: 1205-1317
Time of Attack: 1230
Place of Attack: Pritzwalk area
Height of enemy on first sighting: 500′
Own height at first sighting: 6000′
Was cine gun used: Yes.
Was gyro sight used: Yes.
Our casualties: Nil.
Enemy Casualties: 1 F.W. 190 destroyed by W/Cmdr KEEFER, DSO, DFC

W/Cmdr Keefer states:

I was leading Spinner Blue Section on an Armed Recce when just east of an airfield in the Pritzwalk area Blue 3 reported A/C in the circuit of the airfield. We dived down on them from 6000′ and as we went over the field, more were taking off. I picked out one and fired on him from 30 degrees angle and saw one strike. The E/A turned to Port and I went down to the deck, straightened and flew straight and level. I gave him another burst and got strikes all over him. He crashed into a wood.

I claim this enemy aircraft Destroyed.

F/O Trevorrow confirms this. He says: "I was Blue 2; I saw the W/Cmdr firing at the F.W. 190. The E/A rolled over onto his back, dived into a wood and burst into flames."

SIGNED:
Signature of Pilot: G. Keefer
Signature of Pilot confirming: T.L. Trevorrow.
Signature of Intelligence Officer: R.M. Williams, P/O.

Flying over their new base at Celce, Germany, the Wing swept over Berlin on April 24th and on this occasion met a large formation of Russian aircraft. Circling each other cautiously, the two Allied formations looked each other over and then went their separate ways.

A week later Keefer led the Wing on its last operation of the war when on May 2nd they conducted an uneventful fighter sweep over the Hamburg/Keil area. Two days later the following signal was received from Air Vice Marshall Sir Harry Broadhurst, Air Officer commanding 83 Group:

"Personal for Commanders from A.O.C.: All hostilities on Second Army Front will cease at 0800 hours tomorrow May 5th. Work will continue as usual until orders are issued to the contrary and operational units are to observe strictly the states of availability ordered by the G.C.C."

On the 5th, Keefer left the Wing and arrived in Cannes, France for a two week leave before he returned to Canada. On his return he applied for and was granted his Canadian citizenship. Keefer ended the war with 12 confirmed aerial victories and 5 ground victories and was decorated with the Distinguished Flying Cross and bar and the Distinguished Service Order with Bar. Following is a quote from the citation which accompanied his bar to his DSO: "Since his appointment as Wing Commander Operations, Wing Commander Keefer has led and trained his wing to a high pitch of keenness and efficiency. Under his leadership the Wing has destroyed 191 enemy aircraft and damaged many more. In addition, a great variety of enemy ground targets have been successfully attacked. During this period, Wing Commander Keefer has destroyed four enemy aircraft in the air bringing his total victories to twelve aircraft destroyed. He has also destroyed at least 60 enemy transport vehicles. In April 1945 he completed a daring attack on eleven Me 109s assembled on an airfield at Parchim. Despite intense and accurate anti-aircraft fire the attack was pressed home and all the enemy aircraft were destroyed. This officer has completed three tours of operational duty and has proved himself to be a leader of the highest order and a cool and fearless pilot."

VICTORY CLAIMS

Date:	Enemy Aircraft:		
7 Dec 1941	1 Macchi 200	destroyed	
	1 Macchi 200	damaged	
8 Dec 1941	1 Me 109	damaged	
21 Dec 1941	1 Ju 88	destroyed	
8 Jun 1942	1 Macchi 202	destroyed	
12 Jun 1942	1 Me 109	damaged	
16 Jun 1942	1 Me 109	destroyed	
17 Jun 1942	1 Macchi 202	damaged	
10 Jul 1942	2 Macchi 202s	damaged	
12 Jun 1943	1 FW 190	damaged	
7 Jun 1944	1 Ju 88	destroyed	over Normandy beachhead
	1 FW 190	destroyed	
25 Jun 1944	1 Me 110	destroyed	
27 Jun 1944	1 Me 109	destroyed	
2 Mar 1945	1 Me 109	destroyed	near Rheine
19 Mar 1945	1 Me 109	destroyed	near Rheine
20 Apr 1945	1 Me 109	destroyed	near Wittstock
25 Apr 1945	1 FW 190	destroyed	near Pritzwalk

The Hawker Hurricane II piloted by Keefer while with 274 Squadron and the Spitfire IXB he flew during the Normandy invasion support with 126 wing are illustrated on page 61.

KIPP, Squadron Leader Robert A.
418 Squadron
Royal Canadian Air Force
(10.5 Victories)

Robert Allan Kipp, born on October 12, 1919 in Kamloops, British Columbia, joined the Royal Canadian Air Force in Vancouver on June 27, 1940 and was immediately sent to No. 1 Manning Depot in Toronto, Ontario. He shipped overseas on March 1, 1943 and joined No. 60 Operational Training Unit until November when he was transferred to 418 "City of Edmonton" Squadron (RCAF) flying the deHavilland Mosquito in a night intruder capacity.

At the time Kipp joined the unit, it was experiencing a drop in its sortie output, the main reason being the unpredictable English weather, which was at its worst during the last quarter of the year. Only 141 missions were flown during this time by the unit, half of the previous quarter's output, so Kipp's breaking in period was fairly uneventful, and he was allowed a chance to practice his gunnery skill and completely familiarize himself with the Mosquito. During this time, Kipp did, however, achieve his first taste of aerial combat when on December 12th, he and another Mosquito of the squadron, piloted by F/O Jimmy Johnson combined to destroy a He 111 at Bourges, France during a rare day-ranger insurgent type action. A month later, on January 18, 1944 Kipp and his navigator, F/O Pete Huletsky, both officially on leave according to the Squadron's log, flew an intruder mission to Juvincourt to intercept enemy bombers returning from a raid on the London area. In approximately one minute's time, they made two bomb runs over the enemy field and started bonfires at opposite ends of the landing area. Each of these fires later proved to be a Luftwaffe Me 410 in the process of landing and taking off.

In February, the executive positions of the unit experienced a change, with Wing Commander Macdonald handing over the unit to Wing Commander Dick Bennell. Also departing were two of the squadron's Flight Commanders who were replaced by Howie Cleveland and Kipp. In his new capacity, Kipp led a daylight intrusion which was credited with seven enemy aircraft on April 14th. Assigned to sweep the Kastrup airfield in Copenhagen, Denmark, Kipp sighted four Ju 52s and, with another Mosquito piloted by Johnny Caine, attacked. Each pilot was credited with the destruction of two of the Luftwaffe planes. Kipp then led the flight on a strafing run over the primary target area and three more of the Luftwaffe's planes were destroyed. At this point a pair of Fw 190s appeared from Grove airfield and dived on the Mosquitos. Kipp and his unit turned home and with their speed kept out of the enemy's effective firing range. For his actions and planning of this operation, Kipp was decorated with the Distinguished Flying Cross.

On the 2nd and 3rd of May, 418 Squadron was to establish its 100th victory against the enemy. After the action of the 2nd the unit's total had increased to 96 and all pilots queued up for the chance to bag the 100th. Taking off within minutes of each other during the evening of the 3rd, were the teams of MacFayden-Wright and Kipp-Huletsky. While MacFayden headed for St. Yan, Kipp was assigned to patrol near Munich, Germany. MacFayden was the first to attack that night, destroying a Heinkel, and his chances appeared good for increasing the score as he dived to photograph the area. Suddenly his aircraft was hit by machine-gun fire and he was forced to head home. Kipp, in the meantime, downed four Fw 190s to gain not only the 100th victory, but the 98th, 99th and 101st. The first was illuminated by the beams of searchlights with which it was working near Ammer Lake, the second was approaching to land at Gunzburg with its navigational lights aglow and offered an excellent target, while the third and fourth were flying near Saarburg with full lights in tight formation. The last two were destroyed with a single pass by Kipp. In achieving these four victories, Kipp had not only reached ace status, but had established a RAF-RCAF single night record without the help of Airborne Interception Equipment (radar). He was awarded the Distinguished Service Order for this action.

Until June 1944 most of Kipp's operations consisted of "flowers" (bomber escort missions) over rail targets in France. When unable to find enemy aircraft or lighted airfields to attack, Kipp and the squadron took a vested interest in the destruction of Axis communication by bombing and strafing roads, railyards, and communications installations. Although from the 8th to the 15th of June very few enemy aircraft were seen, on the 14th three were destroyed. The team of Kipp and Huletsky scored one of these, a He 111, during a day-ranger sortie over the Baltic. For Kipp, who was soon to be posted for leave, it was his last victory and increased his total to 10.5 confirmed enemy aircraft destroyed in the air and made him the Squadron's highest scoring ace.

Shortly after 0400 hours on June 13, 1944, the day before Kipp achieved his final victory, while returning over Northern France from an intruder patrol, one of the squadron's pilots sighted what they described as a "rocket projectile heading northward leaving a red trail". At 0418 that morning the first flying bomb fell on England. Occasional sightings by members of the unit followed in the next few days, and because of the devastating effect of this new German weapon on its English targets (for every V-1 that reached England 1.4 people were killed, and 4.1 were seriously injured), 418 Squadron's main responsibility was switched to night intrusion and "flower" sorties to destroy the V-1 Divers (code name) and their launch sites. Kipp flew only a few of these anti-rocket missions before he was ordered to 11 Group Headquarters, where he was posted to a staff position. He remained here until September 7th when he reported to RCAF Overseas Headquarters. Kipp was returned to Canada on July 23, 1945.

The deHavilland Mosquito VI piloted by Kipp with 418 Squadron at Holmsley Hunsdon, Herts, South England in Oct. 1944 is illustrated on page 54.

Special long range reconnaissance Mk. XVI Mosquito had range of 1,370 miles and could reach an altitude of 43,000 ft. while hauling two tons of bombs in its modified bay.

Personal kill markings and nose art on Kipp's Mosquito Mk. VI of 418 Sqdn. RCAF. Swastika marked with number 100, signifies squadron's 100th victory, also garnered by Kipp.

KOBAYASHI, Major Teruhiko
244th Fighter Sentai
Imperial Japanese Army Air Force
(25 Victories)

Teruhiko Kobayashi, born on November 17, 1920 in Kobe, Japan, entered elementary school in Nagasaki in April 1927 where he completed his studies in March 1933. In April he entered middle school in Tokyo for a five year course, however, he did not finish the full term as he left school to enter the Preparatory Military Academy on April 1, 1937. Kobayashi completed this training on August 31, 1938 and a day later entered the Military Academy School. He graduated from there on February 27, 1940 at which time he was assigned to the Army Air Force and was given the probationary rank of a pilot officer.

Through March and June, Kobayashi was assigned to the 45th Sentai in Manchuria, and on May 1st was given the rank of second lieutenant. In July, he was sent to the Kumagaya Army Flying School for additional pilot training, and in May 1941 entered the Noshiro Branch of the Hokota Flying School for training in light bomber tactics. On August 1st he was promoted to the rank of first lieutenant and the following month was posted back to Manchuria to serve with the 66th Sentai.

Kobayashi took part in his first action on December 8, 1941 (December 7th, American) when he piloted a Mitsubishi Ki.21 Type 97 bomber in the raids on Hong Kong. He remained in the China-Manchuria theater until October 1, 1942, when he was sent back to Japan for additional training at the Hokota Flying School as a pursuit pilot.

In March 1943 Kobayashi graduated from Hokota and by April was back with the 66th Sentai in Manchuria near the Russian border. In September, after completing a short course in anti-submarine defense at Kure Naval Air Base, he was assigned to a Submarine Warning Detachment unit operating from Dairen, Manchuria on flights over the Yellow Sea on the east coast of Korea. In November he was reassigned to the Akeno Fighter Training School for advanced fighter training, graduating in April 1944 with the rank of Captain. Kobayashi remained at Akeno through October as a flight instructor, at which time he was posted to the Army Air Base on Shikoku as assistant commander. A month later, in November, Kobayashi was assigned to the 244th Fighter Sentai as Commanding Officer and was given the responsibility of defending the Tokyo area from enemy air attack. His first action as a fighter pilot occurred on December 3rd when a large formation of enemy aircraft penetrated into the Kanto region and the 244th, flying Kawasaki Ki.61s, was ordered to intercept. Kobayashi's aircraft was hit by the guns of one of the American B-29 Superforts and he was forced back to base. However, he mounted a stand-by aircraft and again took to the air. Although not scoring himself, Kobayashi's unit was credited with six planes destroyed and during the aerial battle they actually rammed three of the B-29s with their own aircraft. The result of this ramming strategy cost the 244th two damaged aircraft and one destroyed, however, no pilots were lost.

On January 23, 1945, American B-29s raided Nagoya, and Kobayashi along with three other pilots climbed to 31,000 feet to intercept them over Okazaki. Sighting fifteen planes in the formation at approximately 27,000 feet, Kobayashi ordered the attack and dove at the lead B-29. A cloud of black smoke billowed from the left inside engine. After several passes the enemy plane, now hit in numerous areas, nosed down and spun to the earth below. Returning to base Kobayashi refueled and rearmed his Ki.61 and pursued the formation over the ocean, continuing the attack. The final score for the day's action was six B-29s destroyed and fourteen damaged without the loss of a single pilot from the 244th.

On January 27th the B-29s returned for a raid on Tokyo. At 12:58 p.m. the 244th took off to intercept and at 2:00 sighted the bomber formation flying to the north over the west end of Mount Fujiyama. Attacking the lead aircraft, Kobayashi changed his mind at the last instant (about 300 feet from the B-29) and directed his attack to the second plane in the formation. He impacted against the B-29 and was knocked unconscious. Recovering at approximately 10,000 feet, Kobayashi bailed out of his burning Ki.61 and parachuted safely. The B-29 rammed by Kobayashi, burst into flames around the left engines and left wing root and had its left horizontal stabilizer separated. It nosed over and crashed into the ground.

On May 15th, Kobayashi was promoted to the rank of Major and a week later was assigned to the Chiran Army Air Base in Kyushu to serve as fighter escort for the Kamikaze planes stationed there. The 244th was reassigned on July 15th to the Yokaichi Airbase in Shiga Prefecture to defend against the invasion force expected from the United States Fleet. On July 25th, although ordered to stay on the ground, Kobayashi ordered his men into the air to intercept a formation of Grumman F6F-5s. The 244th circled over their base, and as the Grummans prepared for an expected uneventful strafing run, the Ki.61s and Ki.100s dove to the attack. During the conflict most of the F6Fs were destroyed. However, upon his return to the base, Kobayashi received word from the Army High Command that he was to be court martialed for disobeying direct orders. Fortunately for Kobayashi and

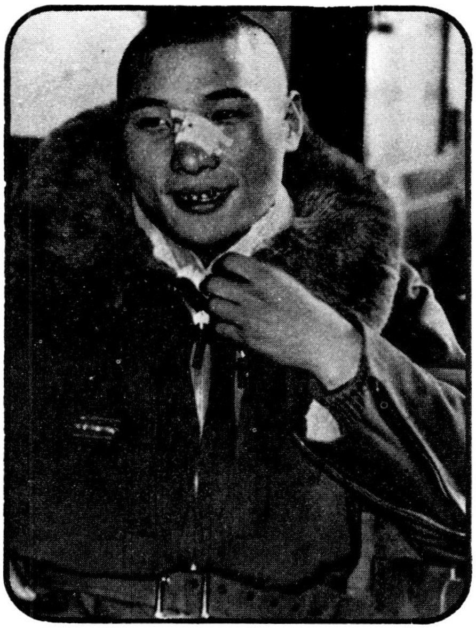

the 244th, Emperor Hirohito heard of the action and commended Kobayashi for his aggressiveness, and the affair was soon forgotten. This proved to be the last action in which Kobayashi was to take part before the end of the war.

Kobayashi was decorated with the Army Valor Award, and received commendations from the Commanding General, Eastern Forces on January 27, 1945, and from His Majesty the Emperor on July 25, 1945. He ended the war with 25 enemy planes to his credit which included 16 American B-29s and 9 fighters. During his tours of duty and training he flew almost every Imperial Japanese Army Air Force aircraft including the Nakajima Ki.43, the Nakajima Ki.44, the Kawasaki Ki.61 fighters, and the Mitsubishi Ki.21 and Nakajima Ki.48 bombers.

Kobayashi's aircraft is illustrated on page 43.

Major Kobayashi's Ki. 61 Tony, flown with 244th Sentai. Engine was 1,500 hp. Kawasaki-built inverted-Vee of twelve cylinders. Right: Kobayashi after he rammed and downed B-29.

Kobayashi and mechanic in front of Kawasaki Tony. Fighter had a top speed of 373 mph., a range of 746 miles at 215 mph., carried a pair of 20mm cannon and two 12.7mm machine guns, plus two 550 lb. bombs. These were deleted in air defense role, the Tony carrying extra ammunition and fuel instead.

KROSCHINSKI, Lt. Hans-Joachim
JG 54
Luftwaffe
(76 Victories)

Hans-Joachin, Kroschinski, born in Gumbinnen, East Prussia, enlisted in the German Luftwaffe in 1937 at Neukuhren. He transferred to flight training after completion of his basic training in 1941 and he was posted to JG 54 on the Russian Front in June 1942, assigned to 2. Staffel in Gatchina. On his second aerial encounter, Kroschinski was credited with his first victory, a MIG-1, while covering the defense zone near Leningrad, south of Lake Ladoga. By December 25th he had destroyed his fifth enemy aircraft and was awarded the Iron Cross.

In the heavy fighting of January and February 1943, Kroschinski increased his total to 14, but shortly after, was transferred to the test center at Rechlin, Germany. Here he flew an Fw 190 testing 210 mm smoke grenade launchers and a parachute guided bomb, both intended for breaking up Allied bomber formations. In May, Kroschinski was returned to JG 54 in Russia, patrolling the southern section of the Kharkov zone, where he increased his score to 25 before being reassigned to Orel, where, in July 1943 he was wounded and forced to parachute from his burning plane. He landed behind his own lines and returned to duty almost immediately.

In September 1943, Kroschinski was posted to IV/JG 54. After only two months with this unit he returned again to 2./JG 54, this time in the central sector of the Gruppe's defense zone. By March 1944 his score stood at 46 and he was posted to instructor duties at Liegnitz. During this training period, Kroschinski often led his students against bomber formations and on Easter Monday 1944 he was credited with destroying his first B-17. In August the training unit was moved to Sagan-Kupper, and in September Kroschinski was again returned to JG 54, flying support for the German troops caught in the Kurland encirclement. He increased his score to 71 by mid-December 1944, but on the 21st, Kroschinski was shot down himself while attacking and destroying 5 Russian Pe-2s. Suffering severe wounds and burns, he finished the war in a German hospital with 76 victories to his credit and received the Knights Cross on April 17, 1945. One of the Me 109s piloted by Kroschinski in Russia is illustrated on page 46 in both its summer and winter camouflage scheme.

Focke-Wulf 190A-8 being put through its paces after WW II. Very maneuverable and fast under 21,000 ft., Fw 190 was an incomparable dogfighter.

LEWIS, Sqdrn. Ldr. Albert G.
249 Squadron
Royal Air Force
(18 Victories)

Albert Gerald Lewis, born on April 10, 1918 in Kimberley, South Africa, received his education at Boys High School and Christian Brothers College in his home town. He enlisted in the Special Service Battalion, South African Infantry at the age of sixteen and after a tour of duty went to work at the Springs Gold Mines. Lewis enlisted in the Royal Air Force at the age of twenty accepting a four-year Short Service Commission and was given the rank of Acting Pilot Officer, effective in October, 1938. He was sent to No. 5 Elementary Flying Training School at Hanwell, England where he flew the Blackburn B-2, and in November was posted to No. 3 Flying Training School at South Cerney in Gloucestershire, flying the Hawker Hart, Audax and Fury. Awarded his wings in March 1939, Lewis was sent to an advanced flying training unit, completing his training in June. On the 15th, Lewis was posted to his first assignment to HMS *Daedalus* with No. 754 Squadron of the Fleet Air Arm (HMS *Daedalus* was a shore base).

On June 20, 1939 Lewis was involved in a flying accident, crashing his Walrus, and was hospitalized until August when he reported back for duty. On September 18th he was transferred to 616 Squadron (South Yorkshire) Auxiliary Air Force flying Gauntlets, Tutors and Battles. Flying a Gauntlet from Doncaster Racecourse, his first mission was one of local reconnaissance. Lewis was shortly posted to No. 12 Group Ferry Pool where he was assigned to ferrying Gloster Gladiators while at the same time continuing practice with the basic RAF fighter tactics.

On December 16, 1939 Lewis was posted to 504 Squadron (City of Nottingham) at Debden. The unit was equipped with the Hawker Hurricane and he was transitioned into the new plane flying short hops between Debden, Duxford and Martlesham Heath. Lewis's first contact with the enemy occurred on January 30, 1940, when, during a shipping patrol mission, he encountered a Luftwaffe Blohm and Voss long-range seaplane, however, no conclusive combat occurred. Lewis flew over 300 hours on convoy patrols, formation practices, night flights, and escort duty with 504 Squadron before being posted to 87 Squadron in France in April 1940. Upon his arrival he was immediately transferred to 85 Squadron under the command of Squadron Leader Oliver. When the "Phony War" ended in May, the unit flew almost dawn to dusk, every day, in support of the British Expeditionary Force and in an effort to halt the German advances. On May 12th, Lewis shot down a Me 109E and a He 111 to account for his first two victories.

On May 19th Lewis was credited with destroying five Luftwaffe aircraft in a single day. Piloting a Hurricane I, coded AK-A, he shot down two Me 109s on the morning patrol and accounted for three more during his evening sortie. On the evening mission Lewis was flying near the French-Belgian border in the Roubaix area where he was jumped by a flight of three Me 109s. About to return to his base, he was unaware of the enemy aircraft until tracers began to pass by his wing. Turning to face the attack, Lewis found himself in a straight-on course with the Luftwaffe flight leader. As the distance closed, the Me 109 suddenly rolled into a steep turn as he tried to pull away. Lewis pressed home the attack into the exposed belly of the enemy aircraft which began burning and continued its dive into the earth below. The remaining two Me 109s broke off the encounter and headed for their base with Lewis in pursuit. Following the two fighters, Lewis pulled up slightly below and behind them, firing a short burst into each of the tightly grouped planes. Lewis watched as each turned into a steep dive and exploded as they disappeared into the forest below.

On his return to his base at Seclin, Lewis was told that the action had been confirmed by both British ack-ack crews, and by various other ground witnesses, and that he was being recommended for the Distinguished Flying Cross. That evening, Lewis and 85 Squadron evacuated the base at Seclin and flew to Merville where two days later, on May 21st the RAF component was withdrawn to England. Lewis flew one of only sixty-six serviceable Hurricanes left of the Expeditionary Force Air Component, landing at Gatwick, and later flying to Northholt through balloon cables.

Lewis was back in action in early June. On the 14th he flew a Hurricane on an operational patrol over the Channel, and on the following day was assigned a reconnaissance mission in the Boulogne, Arras, Amiens, Abbeville area. In late June Lewis flew to Castle Camps from Debden (Castle Camps becoming 85 Squadron's flying base during the early stages of the Battle of Britain). The leader of 85 Squadron at this time was Peter Townsend (later to become a Group Captain). It was Townsend who pinned the nickname "Zulu" on Lewis because of his South Africa heritage.

On July 1, 1940, operations for 85 Squadron became continual and in deadly earnest. Lewis began flying three and four missions a day. These missions usually being of a convoy escort and patrol type from his base at Martlesham Heath. Lewis accounted for a Me 110 while flying solo patrol on August 18th and shortly after, moved with the Squadron to their new base at Croydon. From here, on August 31st, Lewis destroyed a Me 109E after he had been scrambled with eight other Hurricanes to patrol around Hawkinge. They were ordered to intercept a formation of Luftwaffe Me 109s over Dover at approximately 15,000 feet. Circling out to sea, the flight of Hurricanes turned in from behind the enemy planes and with a short burst from 150 yards, Lewis flamed one of them. On this mission four of the nine enemy fighters were destroyed without loss to 85 Squadron.

Through August and into September, Lewis continued operational sorties with 85 Squadron until on September 5th he moved to Church Fenton in Yorkshire where he was assigned to routine patrols until September 15th. On this day, Lewis was posted to 249 Squadron at North Weald. In 249 Squadron he was greeted by several other South Africans, among them, Pat Wells, Jimmy Crossey, and Percy Burton. With this unit Lewis quickly got back into the thick of battle,

again flying three to five missions in a single day. On his first day with his new Squadron, Lewis was credited with a He 111 and shared in the probable destruction of a second. Three days later, on September 18th, Lewis achieved his twelfth confirmed victory of the war, and on September 27th was credited with the destruction of six confirmed and three probable enemy aircraft to raise his total score to eighteen.

The following day, September 28th, Lewis was on patrol over Maidstone when he was jumped by a Me 109 and was shot down. Covering the main body of the Squadron from above, he was hit from behind and his aircraft set afire. He parachuted from the burning plane with fellow South African Jimmy Crossey circling and following him down to ensure he was not shot at while in his harness. Lewis landed safely on the ground, but had suffered severe burns and was immediately taken to Faversham Cottage Hospital. He lost his sight for a time and was treated for burns on his hands, legs, and face.

Spending two months in the hospital, during which time he was promoted to the rank of Flying Officer, Lewis returned to 249 Squadron in December 1940. He became "A" Flight Commander upon his return and took to the air again on January 17, 1941. He continued flying with 249 Squadron until June on local reconnaissance, night fighter and sweep missions at which time he was transferred to No. 52 Operational Training Unit.

Sqdn. Leader Lewis in the cockpit of his Hurricane, with 85 Squadron, during Battle of Britain. At time, Lewis was a Pilot Officer.

Assigned as an instructor and commander of "C" Flight, Lewis was promoted to Flight Lieutenant in November and for the first time since he joined the RAF piloted the Supermarine Spitfire in addition to Masters, Magisters, Tiger Moths, and Hurricanes. His Commanding Officer at No. 52, OTU was Wing Commander John Grandy, under whom Lewis had previously served during part of his tour with 249 Squadron.

Lewis volunteered for overseas combat duty, and finally in January 1942, was posted to 261 Squadron. He was sent to Takoradi in Sierra Leone, the assembly point for aircraft being flown to the Middle East, and on February 4th left there for Lagos, Nigeria with eighteen Hurricanes. Flying to Kano, to Maiduguri, Nigeria; to El Genina, to Khartoum and finally to Port Sudan, Lewis managed to get all the aircraft to their destination without a loss, covering over 3,000 miles in less than three days.

While in Port Sudan, Lewis was given a chance to fly the Curtiss P-40 Kittyhawk and although he was somewhat impressed by the aircraft's armament and overall performance, he stated after the test hop that he still preferred his Hurricane.

On February 19, 1942, Lewis was shuttled to Headquarters Middle East (HQME) in Cairo, along with Rear-Admiral Denis Boyd, for high level staff meetings, returning to Port Sudan on the next day. He immediately boarded HMS *Indomitable* and put to sea. He flew a Hurricane from her deck destined for China Bay, Ceylon, but was forced to return due to engine trouble

Mainstay of R.A.F. fighter command during Battle of Britain was solid, dependable Hawker Hurricane Mk. I. Armed with eight .30 caliber machine guns (same as the Spitfire) Hurricane was slower, with a top speed of 324 mph., but a very stable gun platform, carrying nearly 2,700 rounds of ammunition.

and made one of the few carrier landings without an arrester hook. His plane was quickly repaired and Lewis finally arrived at Trincomalee in China Bay, Ceylon to take command of 261 Squadron. Most of his new unit was made up of Australian and New Zealand pilots with a scattering of Canadians, and the base itself was quite primitive consisting only of a few thatch huts and a grass runway strip. Dissatisfied with the conditions at the base, Lewis rotated Flights to Batikaloa, near Jafna, which offered more adequate facilities for combat operations.

On April 9, 1942, Lewis was leading the Squadron on an interception mission to stop an incoming Japanese bomber formation. As he was preparing to take off, his plane was strafed by the Japanese fighter escort and Lewis was wounded in the left arm. His aircraft on fire, barely off the ground, Lewis bailed out at only 200 feet, and luckily his parachute opened in time. He landed in the jungle growth below, and lay bleeding for six hours before friendly natives finally found him and returned him to his base.

In June he was returned to England, via South Africa, and was made the Chief Flying Instructor at Tealing in Scotland, and from there was posted to 10 Group Headquarters at Box in Wiltshire. For Lewis, the combat of World War II was over.

Lewis ended the war with eighteen confirmed victories and three probables and was decorated with the Distinguished Flying Cross and Bar. One of the Hurricanes piloted by Lewis as part of "A" Flight with 249 Squadron is illustrated on page 49.

MCCUDDIN, Lt. Leo B.
VF-20
USS Enterprise
USN
(6 Victories)

Leo Bob McCuddin attended public schools in Fallon, Nevada and attended the University of Nevada in Reno where he graduated in 1939. He entered the University of Arizona to study law, but broke off his studies on April 17, 1941 when he was appointed an aviation cadet in the Naval Reserve. He received his flight training at the Naval Air Station, Pensacola, Florida, was commissioned an Ensign on April 2, 1942, and designated a naval aviator on May 22, 1942.

McCuddin was assigned to VF-20 which was commissioned at U.S. Naval Air Station, San Diego, California on October 15, 1943. The unit spent several months receiving advanced training in the F6F-3 fighter and on April 16, 1944 embarked on board the USS *Essex* for the Hawaiian area. Arriving at NAS Barber's Point on April 21st, McCuddin received specialized training in rocket runs and team flying. Finally, on August 4th, he embarked on the USS *Enterprise* for a shakedown cruise in Hawaiian waters, and from there departed for Eniwetok arriving August 21st. McCuddin entered combat for the first time on August 31st taking part in fighter sweeps against Chichi Island in the Bonin chain. During the next few days, he was involved in the strikes against Ani and Naha islands in the same area. On September 6th, he took part in the strikes against Yap Island and a few days later supported the air attacks covering the invasion of Peleliu. In this action, and the followup raids on Malakai, McCuddin received his first experience with the use of napalm.

On October 10th he took part in the initial air strikes against both Yontan and Naha airfields, however, here again, no enemy air opposition was encountered. The first enemy air resistance occurred on October 12th, when McCuddin was involved in action against the Japanese forces over Southern Formosa. Approximately thirty Oscars and Zeros rose to intercept the Allied force. Eighteen of the enemy were shot down without a single loss, and McCuddin was credited with his first two victories. For this action he was awarded the Distinguished Flying Cross.

The strikes against Luzon, October 15th through 18th, were devoted to the destruction of enemy aircraft both on the ground and in the air. McCuddin, escorting bombers to their targets on Nielson and Nichols Fields, Manila, was one of a group of sixteen fighters who had taken off from the *Enterprise*. After having completed his cover duty, McCuddin headed toward the rally point at Laguna de Bay. As he approached the lake, he identified a Japanese Oscar in the base of a cloud front, preparing to dive on a lone TBM Avenger. McCuddin jettisoned his belly tank and climbed with full power toward the enemy plane, forcing the Oscar to break off his attack. McCuddin fired a short burst into the cockpit of the Oscar as it passed in front of him. As the aircraft burst into flames the Japanese pilot bailed out. For this action, McCuddin was awarded the Air Medal.

On October 18th, McCuddin was part of the flight which was assigned fighter sweep duty over Clark Field, Luzon. Strong fighter opposition was encountered by VF-20 on this day from the defending Japanese airmen. Twenty-seven enemy planes were destroyed by VF-20 for the loss of one F6F and its pilot, Ensign William Foye. In this encounter, McCuddin after completing a strafing run, spotted a flight of Japanese Tojos above and behind his F6F-5. Pulling up into a firing position McCuddin fired a burst from his six .50 caliber guns into the first aircraft's cockpit and it burst into flames. Turning into a second Tojo, he fired a burst into the fuselage and it too exploded in flames, crashing to the earth below.

Victor of Pacific War was F6F Hellcat. This one catches wire barrier on USS *Intrepid*. Pratt & Whitney engine of 2000 hp. gave Hellcat a top speed of 386 mph. Drop tank of 140 gallons extended range to 1530 miles.

McCuddin's next combat occurred a week later on the 24th and 25th when he participated in the Second Battle of the Philippine Sea. In this engagement VF-20 engaged in concentrated attacks on three enemy task forces. On the 24th, the unit engaged an enemy formation in the Sulu Sea and the Sibuyan Sea. Carrying only rockets and .50 caliber machine guns, the F6Fs attacked an enemy aircraft carrier and two destroyers. One of the destroyers was sunk and the other two ships damaged without the loss of a single aircraft.

On the 25th, the unit attacked the enemy task force, located in the northeast Luzon area, consisting of four aircraft carriers and two *Iso* class Battleships. The result of this attack was the sinking of one ship and the damaging of three others. For his part in this action, McCuddin was awarded the Navy Cross and the Silver Star Medal. His citations stated that in the face of withering antiaircraft fire, he conducted a devastating rocket attack on major units of the Japanese Fleet and, by his determination and courage, succeeded in scoring direct hits on a hostile destroyer and battleship. His attacks assisted directly in the exploding and sinking of the destroyer and the serious damaging of the battleship.

During the following month, November 1944, McCuddin participated in the Leyte Operations (October 27th through 29th), attacks on the Japanese convoy at Ormac Bay (November 11th), strikes on the Manila Bay and Clark Field areas (November 13th and 14th), and strikes on enemy shipping in Subic Bay (November 19th).

On November 23rd, McCuddin was transferred to the USS *Lexington*, and for a period of two weeks was engaged in organizing new assignments and taking part in a shakedown cruise. In January 1945, he participated in support sweeps for the landings in Lingayen Gulf. Although the sweeps were not directed at the landing area in particular, they were all intended to keep the enemy bottled up and busy in other nearby locations. McCuddin also flew strikes against Southern Formosa, the French Indo-China Coast, Pescadores, Hong Kong and Okinawa.

On February 2nd, VF-20 was transferred to the USS *Kwajalein* and on the 3rd left Ulithi enroute to Guam. From here McCuddin returned to Pearl Harbor and then to San Diego.

McCuddin ended the war with six confirmed aerial victories, seven enemy aircraft destroyed on the ground and was credited with participating in the sinking or damaging of seven enemy ships. One of the F6F-5 Hellcats piloted by McCuddin while on the USS *Enterprise* is illustrated on page 47.

MCGUIRE, Major Thomas B.
431st Fighter Squadron
475th Fighter Group
5th Air Force
(38 Victories)

Thomas McGuire, from Ridgewood, New Jersey, entered the U.S. Army as a Aviation Cadet on July 12, 1941 after studying at Georgia Tech University. He received his primary pilot training at Corsicana, Texas and his basic at Randolph Field, He moved to Kelly Field, Texas for his advanced training and was commissioned as a second lieutenant in February 1942. During the next twelve months, McGuire spent time with the Alaskan Defense Command and trained in the newly available P-38 Lightning before being posted to the 49th Fighter Group in Australia on March 14, 1943. In late July he was reassigned to the 431st Fighter Squadron, 475th Fighter Group and on his first combat mission with this unit on August 18, 1943 was credited with destroying three Japanese aircraft over Wewak. Three days later, on August 21st, McGuire destroyed two more enemy fighters to reach ace status.

On November 1, 1944, McGuire was credited with a "Tojo" while leading his flight to Morotai, for his twenty-fifth victory. Based at Boroka Airfield, Biak Island, Dutch New Guinea, McGuire continued to score frequently and by the end of the year was pressing Richard Bong for the most number of enemy aircraft destroyed. During the next two months McGuire added thirteen more Japanese planes to his score bringing his war ending total to thirty-eight. Following is a capsule summary of these victories, including aircraft type flown, mission, and type and number of aircraft destroyed.

After a week's rest during the first part of January 1945, McGuire returned to active combat. With the Allies on the offensive and with Major Bong returned to the United States, McGuire felt that this was the time he would catch and pass Bong in total victories, however, this was not to be, and on January 7, 1945, McGuire flew his final mission. At dawn, McGuire accompanied by three other pilots of the 431st Fighter Squadron (Captain R. Weaver, Lt. Thropp; and Major Rittmayer) took off for a fighter sweep mission over Fabrica

Date	Aircraft	Mission	Type and Number Aircraft Destroyed
10 Nov 44	P-38L	Escort	1 Nakajima Ki.43 destroyed
12 Nov 44	P-38L	Patrol	2 Mitsubishi J2M3s destroyed
7 Dec 44	P-38L	Support Patrol	1 Nakajima Ki.43 destroyed 1 Nakajima Ki.44 destroyed
13 Dec 44	P-38L	Fighter Sweep	1 Mitsubishi J2M3 destroyed
25 Dec 44	P-38L	Escort	3 Mitsubishi A6M2s destroyed
26 Dec 44	P-38L	Escort	4 Mitsubishi A6M2s destroyed

Right: One of several "Pudgy" P-38s flown by McGuire, shows 17 victories. Left: McGuire and Colonel Charles Lindbergh, who flew combat with 431st Fighter Sqdn. and showed its members how to get maximum range out of the P-38.

Field on Negros Island. Flying at approximately 10,000 feet in light cloud cover the group arrived at Negros at about 7:00 and proceeded to decrease their altitude until they reached 1500 feet in a position just north of the field. Having encountered no enemy aircraft in the area during a loiter period, McGuire gave the order to proceed to the western coast of the island.

Just off the coastline, a lone Mitsubishi A6M3 "Hamp" Zero-Sen was sighted below the group and flying directly toward it. McGuire, followed by the flight of four P-38s peeled off to intercept the Japanese plane, McGuire's aircraft still carrying its drop tanks. At this time, the enemy pilot, aware of the pending danger from above, also conducted some aerial manuevers of his own which placed him directly in a firing position for the aircraft of Lt. Thropp.

McGuire noticing the vulnerability of his flight, turned his P-38 at full power and in the process stalled out. Too low to parachute, McGuire tried in vain to right his plane, but failed. He crashed into the beach below. The existence of heavy Japanese ground fire may also have contributed to McGuire's untimely demise, as during the aerial dogfight it had increased considerably. Nevertheless McGuire had repeatedly warned his pilots never to attempt high G turns at low levels in the P-38, particularly with external tanks.

McGuire flew over 700 combat hours in P-38s and was decorated with the Congressional Medal of Honor for his actions. The aircraft he piloted between November 1944 and January 1945, although not the plane in which he was killed, is illustrated on page 50.

P-38J Lightning, Philippines, June, 1945. Lightning had tremendous range, and with 600 gallons in external tanks, shown here, could fly 2,260 miles at 186 mph. Armament was one 20mm cannon and four .50 caliber machine guns, all in the nose. Speed: 414 mph. at 25,000 ft.

MCNAIR, Wing Commander Robert W.
403 Squadron
Royal Canadian Air Force
(16 Victories)

Robert Wendell "Buck" McNair was born in May 1919 in Springfield, Nova Scotia, and joined the Royal Canadian Air Force in June 1940 receiving his flight training at No. 1 Training School in Toronto, Ontario, No.7 Elementary Flying School in Windsor, Ontario, and No. 31 Flying Training School at Kingston. On May 12, 1941, McNair won his wings and was posted to England where he was assigned to No. 58 Operational Training Unit where he remained until June 23rd at which time he was transferred to 411 Squadron of the RCAF which was in its initial stages of forming. Piloting a Spitfire V, McNair experienced his first combat and achieved his first victory while with this unit when on October 13, 1941 he was credited with destroying an Me 109E while on a fighter sweep over the coast of France.

McNair remained with 411 Squadron until February when he was reposted to the Isle of Malta and assigned to duty with 249 Squadron of the Royal Air Force. No. 249 Squadron had just received the first Spitfires to operate outside of England. The aircraft had been ferried from England on board the Carrier HMS *Eagle* and flown to the island fortress. On March 20, 1942 McNair was credited with his second victory, his first with 249 Squadron, when the unit intercepted a formation of Luftwaffe bombers and McNair flamed one of the escorting Me 109s. He remained on Malta until June 19th when he was transferred back to 411 Squadron in England. During his three and a half month stay with 249 Squadron, McNair reached ace status and was decorated with the Distinguished Flying Cross. His citation read "that this skillful and courageous pilot invariably pressed home his attacks with the greatest determination irrespective of the odds." Following is a list of his claims while on Malta:

DATE	CLAIM
18 March 1942	1 Me 109 damaged
20 March 1942	1 Me 109 destroyed
26 March 1942	1 Ju 88 destroyed
	2 Ju 88s damaged
	1 Me 109 probably destroyed
20 April 1942	1 Me 109 destroyed
	1 Ju 88 damaged
25 April 1942	2 Me 109s damaged
	1 Ju 87 damaged
	1 Ju 88 damaged
22 May 1942	1 Me 109 destroyed
25 May 1942	1 Me 109 destroyed
10 June 1942	1 Me 109 destroyed

McNair remained with 411 Squadron for only two and a half months accounting for his eighth victory before he was given leave and returned to Canada in September 1942. After six months of rest and advanced flight instruction in new tactics and aircraft, he returned to England and in April 1943 was assigned to 403 "Wolf" Squadron of the RCAF stationed at Kenley, Middlesex. Promoted to the rank of Flight Commander, McNair stayed only a short time with 403 Squadron, being posted to 421 "Red Indian" Squadron as a Squadron Leader on June 19th. Piloting a Spitfire IX, McNair accounted for his ninth victory the following day when he destroyed a Focke-Wulf 190A over

Spitfire Mk. IX (MH434) which completed 72 operational sorties in WW II, privately owned and now based at Booker in Buckinhamshire, England displays maneuverability that was Spit's forte. (Stuart Howe)

Dieppe while assigned to bomber escort duty.

McNair flew as a Squadron Leader with 421 Squadron until October 16, 1943 and during this period increased his total score to sixteen. Following is a list of McNair's claims while attached to 421 Squadron.

DATE	CLAIM
20 June 1942	1 FW 190 destroyed
24 June 1942	1 FW 190 destroyed south of Pecamp
6 July 1942	1 Me 109 destroyed north of Amiens
9 July 1942	1 Me 109 damaged near Thielt
10 July 1942	1 Me 109 destroyed near Bernay
31 Aug 1942	1 Me 109 destroyed south of Ghent
3 Sept 1942	1 Me 109 destroyed north of Evreux
5 Sept 1942	1 Me 109 damaged near Deynes
6 Sept 1942	1 FW 190 destroyed near Beaumont le Roger
3 Oct 1942	1 FW 190 destroyed near Heusen

His final victory on October 16, 1943 proved to be a costly one for McNair as he himself was shot down. His Spitfire hit, and on fire, he bailed out over the English Channel. He safely parachuted into the cold water, but the flames surrounding his cowl and cockpit had inflicted their damage before he could get out. His face badly burned, McNair spent two weeks in a hospital and was released. Unknown to him or the doctors who treated him, McNair's eyes had been affected.

He returned to duty on October 17th as Wing Commander of 126 Wing, 83 Group, 2 TAF, which comprised 401 "Ram", 411 "Grizzly Bear" and 412 "Falcon" Squadrons all of the Royal Canadian Air Force. He continued to fly in active combat for a period of six months, but as time progressed he experienced increasing difficulty in focusing and overall depth perception. Finally, on April 12, 1942 he was forced to give up combat flying because of his failing sight and was assigned to ground operations with 17 Wingwhere he remained until July 12, 1944 when he returned to Canada for the rest of the war.

In addition to the Distinguished Service Order, McNair was awarded the Croix de Guerre with Palm and was made a Chevalier of the Legion of Honor. The Spitfire IXb flown by McNair while attached to 403 "Wolf" Squadron in April 1943 at Kenley, Middlesex, England is illustrated on page 62.

MH434

MH434

MCWHORTER, Lt. Cmdr. Hamilton
VF-12
USS Randolph
USN
(12 Victories)

Hamilton McWhorter was born on February 8, 1921 in Athens, Georgia, and attended public schools there. He enrolled at the University of Georgia in Athens and entered the Navy on June 19, 1941 in the V5 AVCAD program at NRAB Atlanta, receiving his flight training at Pensacola from August to December. He was then sent to NAS Miami until February 1942 when he was commissioned and assigned to VF-9 at NAS Norfolk, Virginia. His first combat occurred on November 8, 1942 while flying from the deck of the USS *Ranger*, when he took part in the North African Invasion strafing at Casa Blanca against Vichy French destroyers. After this action, McWhorter and VF-9 were transferred to the USS *Essex* for duty with Westpac. He reentered combat in May 1943 and was credited with his first aerial victory (a Zero) on October 5th over Wake Island.

On November 11th McWhorter took part in the action against Rabaul escorting torpedo and dive bombers striking enemy shipping in the harbor. Returning from the mission he sighted a dogfight over the harbor area and climbed to investigate. The action included a dozen F6Fs and about forty Zeros. McWhorter destroyed two of the enemy before his own aircraft was crippled and he was forced to return to the USS *Essex* with two Zeros on his tail. On this day, VF-9 had its best day scoring 55 victories for the loss of only one pilot. In May 1944 McWhorter was transferred to VF-12 aboard the USS *Randolph* and finished the war with this unit.

McWhorter flew 86 combat missions and over 290 combat hours taking part in the strikes on Marcus Island, Wake Island, Rabaul, Gilbert Islands, Kwajalein, Marshall Islands, Saipan, Truk, Iwo Jima, Okinawa and the first raids on Tokyo. His final score stood at 12 victories and he was decorated with five Distinguished Flying Crosses and seven Air Medals. The F6F Hellcat flown by McWhorter while serving with VF-12 on the USS *Randolph* is illustrated on 47.

A flight of Grumman F6F Hellcats rev up prior to launch from deck of USS *Lexington* (CV-12) February, 1945.

OLDS, Major Robin
434th Fighter Squadron
479th Fighter Group
8th Air Force
(13 Victories)

Robin Olds was born in Honolulu, Hawaii on July 14, 1922, the son of Major General Robert Olds, but spent the majority of his early years in Hampton, Virginia where he attended both elementary and high school. He entered the United States Military Academy in July of 1940. While a cadet at West Point he received primary training at the Spartan School of Aviation in Tulsa, Oklahoma, and both his basic and advanced flight training at Stewart Field, New York. Olds received his wings on May 30, 1943 and graduated from the Point two days later. He was sent to fighter tactics school for nine months, after which he was assigned to the 434th Fighter Squadron which had been activated on October 15, 1943. Olds received additional training in the Lockheed P-38, and in May was shipped overseas with the unit on board the USS *Argentina*. He arrived in England on May 14, 1944 and the unit took up residence at RAF Wattisham, where they remained for the duration of the war.

He flew his first combat mission in May 1944 and was credited with his first aerial victories on August 14th when he downed two FW-190s in the skies over Montmiral, France. On February 7, 1945, Olds was promoted to Major and in March was given command of the 434th, a position he held until the end of the war. Although he began his tour in the ETO flying a P-38 Lightning (SCAT I) he soon found himself piloting P-51 Mustangs, finishing the war in a D model (SCAT VII). Olds flew 107 missions and was credited with a total of twenty-four and a half victories, thirteen in the air (nine in P-38s) and eleven and a half on the ground. Among the many decorations he received were the Distinguished Flying Cross, the Silver Star, the British Distinguished Flying Cross, and the French Croix de Guerre. Immediately after the war, Olds began flying P-80 jets at March Air Force Base and was part of the USAF's first acrobatic team. A career officer, Olds later distinguished himself as commandant of the Air Force Academy and, during the last several years, by his service in Vietnam. He retired in 1973 with the rank of general.

One of the P-51 Mustangs flown by Olds while commander of the 434th is illustrated on page 33. It was the sixth aircraft flown by him to carry the nickname SCAT.

The consummate fighting/flying machine of WW II, North American's P-51D Mustang. Top speed: 437 mph. at 25,000 ft. Range: (clean) 950 miles at an exceptionally fast cruise of 395 mph. (1300 miles at 260 mph.). These range/speed parameters made the P-51 the finest escort fighter of the war, enabling it to reach most targets, fight and return. Range of 2,080 miles could be achieved with two 100 gallon drop tanks, at 244 mph.

PURDY, Captain John E.
433rd Fighter Squadron
475th Fighter Group
5th Air Force
United States Air Force
(7 Victories)

P-38L was final production Lightning. Of 10,560 built, 3,810 were attack models like this one. L was first to mount tree type rocket launchers carrying 5-inch rockets. Shown here is prototype.

John E. Purdy was born in Detroit, Michigan on June 17, 1919, but moved to Wyandotte, Michigan at an early age, the town he was to call home during the war. He was drafted in June 1941 and sent to Ft. Riley, Kansas for cavalry training. He was transferred to Ft. Snelling, Minnesota in October where he remained until Pearl Harbor, when he applied for assignment to the Flying Cadets. On the acceptance of his request, Purdy was sent to Santa Ana, California for his pre-flight training, and then to Mira Loma Flight Academy at Oxnard, California for his primary. He completed his basic at Gardner Field, Taft, California and his advanced training at Luke Field, Arizona. Training in P-40s, P-39s and P-38s with the 4th Fighter Command, Purdy was placed on active service on May 20, 1943 and assigned overseas duty on December 14th as a replacement pilot in the 475th Fighter Squadron based at Buna, New Guinea.

Purdy started his combat flying on December 30th when he was assigned a patrol and search mission in a P-38H near Gloucester. During the following months he flew a variety of search, cover, patrol and escort duty until on May 16, 1944 he was credited with destroying his first enemy plane while on escort duty with B-24 Liberators over Noemfoor Island. Assigned a P-38L in November 1944, Purdy was credited with his next two victories on December 5th while on patrol duty near Leyte. On this day he was leading a flight of four P-38s on patrol over the Albuera Plaridel area on the west coast of Leyte Island. Near the city of Cebu at an altitude of 8000 feet the flight spotted a formation of six Val dive bombers and Purdy immediately ordered an attack. He destroyed two of the enemy, sending them crashing into the ground north of the city, but as his flight turned for home it was attacked from above by ten Japanese Oscars vectoring on the rear of his formation. Purdy immediately turned his P-38 to the attack, dispersing the enemy planes, but the Oscars mounted a second attack on the flight and again Purdy flew head long into their midst, firing short bursts. This time the enemy broke off and turned for their home base.

Purdy scored his fourth and fifth victories on December 11th while on escort duty with a PBY from Tacloban to Ormoc Bay on Leyte Island. At 0900 hours flying at 3000 feet, fifteen miles north of Cebu Island, he sighted a

convoy moving south and at the same time six enemy aircraft north of the convoy at an altitude of 12,000 feet. The PBY was ordered back to its base and Purdy then led his flight in a climb in preparation for an attack. During the climb, thirty more enemy planes were sighted at altitudes of 5000 to 7000 feet. Ignoring the superiority of the enemy formation, Purdy attacked an Oscar at 7000 feet which was later claimed as damaged. Firing a burst at 200 yards from 80° deflection on another Oscar, Purdy watched as it burst into flame and crashed into the sea north of Bantayan Island. Noticing two Oscars closing on his second element, Purdy turned to meet their attack and firing from 50 yards flamed the leading plane and sent it crashing to the sea. During this battle which lasted over twenty minutes, Purdy's flight was credited with destroying five of the enemy without suffering a loss, however, Purdy's plane ran out of fuel and he was forced to ditch south of Leyte being picked up by an American Catalina.

On the afternoon of December 17th Purdy, with a new aircraft, was leading Blue Flight, thirteen P-38s, assigned to patrol the beachhead on Mindoro Island. At 1625 two Zero 52 type fighters were sighted at 9000 feet heading northeast about four miles east of Nagaran. Satisfied that they had not been observed by the American flight, the two Zeros remained on their course. Purdy broke off and gained altitude in preparation for an attack and selected the right hand plane for his first pass. Twenty millimeter shells exploded against the fuselage and canopy as the Zero fell to the mountains below. Purdy quickly turned his attention to the second Zero and fired a short burst from 10° deflection setting the plane afire. The pilot bailed out as the aircraft spun into the island.

On January 9, 1945 Purdy was conducting a routine dive bombing mission on a bridge in the Luzon area; but as he closed over the target with only 200 feet between him and ground zero, his aircraft was hit by ground fire. He climbed to 5000 feet before he noticed his left engine had quit. He then discovered he had lost his controls and was unable to trim. It was still too low to bail out so Purdy guided the crippled craft over an area which American Intelligence had designated as controlled by Philippine guerrillas and crashed into a small knoll. He was taken from the wreckage by men under the command of General Patrico Erne and his wounds were treated.

After two weeks of rest, contact was made with American Intelligence working with the guerillas and Purdy joined the intelligence officer at his headquarters. They started for the coast where the pick up by American Forces was arranged. As they passed through a town of about 4000 inhabitants, a parade was given in Purdy's honor by 200 guerilla troops who lined the streets and presented arms. A band played the American National Anthem as Purdy and the intelligence officer rode white horses behind a bodyguard of Philippino veterans of Bataan and the U.S. Navy.

After a month's rest, Purdy returned to duty on March 29, 1945 flying an escort patrol with B-24s to Indochina. He continued flying until May 16th at which time he had completed 143 missions and 484 combat flight hours.

The P-38L piloted by Purdy in late December 1944 is illustrated on page 51.

RALL, Major Guenther
JG 52
Luftwaffe
(275 Victories)

Guenther Rall, born in Gaggenau Baden on March 10, 1918 the son of a storekeeper, received his primary education in his home town and was an ardent member of the German Boy Scouts. He was exposed to woodcrafts, camping, and other normal scouting activities, but had no contact with the aviation world during his early years. He completed school in 1936 and joined the German Army. After finishing his infantry training, Rall was sent to the War College in Dresden for officer's instruction and decided that aviation was his real career, transferring to the Luftwaffe pilots' school at Neudieburg in the summer of 1938. From here he was sent to Gunnery School at Werneuchen, near Berlin where he was trained under the leadership of pilots who had already achieved ace status in the Spanish Civil War.

Rall was given a commission as a Second Lietutenant and assigned to II Gruppe of Jagdgeschwader 52 near Stuttgart in late 1939. He started his operational flying on patrol missions along the German-French border as the youngest officer in the unit, but combat with the French reconnaissance aircraft was rare and when it did occur, Rall was unfortunate enough to be always in another area. Shortly after the invasion of France in May 1940, a third Gruppe was formed in JG 52 and Rall was posted to the 8th Staffel of this unit at Mannheim. On May 12th, his Staffel was ordered to escort a Luftwaffe reconnaissance plane returning from a sortie over France and as the German fighters sighted their aircraft, it was attacked by a formation of French Curtiss P-36s. The Luftwaffe flight dove to its rescue and in the fight Rall scored his first victory. For the rest of the month it was more sorties and more victories for both Rall and JG 52. Then in June the unit was recalled to a base on the North Sea where its aircraft were modified for overwater flights and its pilots trained in the art of ditching and survival at sea. From there III Gruppe was sent to a base near Calais, France to take part in the Battle of Britain.

Rall remained with III Gruppe until its withdrawal in October 1940, at which time the unit was allowed to replenish the severe losses it had suffered during the months of July and August. Then, while the Gruppe moved to a new base in Vienna, Austria, Rall and the 8th Staffel were posted to Bucharest, Rumania to protect the oil refineries and pipelines there, as well as several key bridges across the Danube. The next two months passed uneventfully, but this ended in May 1941 when Rall's Staffel was sent to support the attack on Crete. Following the fall of the island on May 27, 1941, the 8th Staffel returned to Rumania where it remained during June and July taking to the air against the heavy bombers of the Soviet Air Force in defense of the Rumanian refineries in the Constanza area, which was feeding the war machine of Germany. In one five day period, June 23rd to June 28th, Rall and his unit accounted for over forty of the Soviet aircraft.

From Rumania Rall's unit moved to Southern Russia to join up with other units of JG 52 who were covering the offensive push by the German ground forces from the Crimea to the Sea of Azov. In the battle for Rostov, Rall scored steadily and by November 28, 1941 had run his total victory score to thirty-six enemy aircraft. On this day Rall was returning to his base when he engaged a flight of Soviet fighters over German held territory and in the ensuing dogfight was shot down. He crash landed his Me 109F in an open field, but was flung forward by the impact striking his head on the instrument panel. He was pulled from the wreckage and transported to a field hospital by friendly troops, but suffered temporary paralysis from a broken back. Rall remained in a Bucharest hospital until December and was then transferred to Vienna where he stayed until August 1942, when he rejoined JG 52 at Tagaenrog, Russia. Rall went back into combat more aggressive than ever and on October 22nd was credited with his 100th victory. For the next several months Rall took part in the battles around Caucasus, Stalingrad, Kuban, and Novorossisk. His score continued to climb and on August 29, 1943 he became the third Luftwaffe pilot to achieve 200 victories. On November 28th he became only the second to reach 250.

Early in 1944 Rall was transferred to Jagdeschwader 11 to command II Gruppe on the Western Front. This was a high altitude interceptor unit formed to engage the fighter escort of Allied bomber formations. Rall added three more victories to his credit with this unit before he was again shot down and wounded on May 12th. On this occasion his aircraft was hit by an American P-47 and Rall was hit in the left hand by one of the exploding shells. He remained hospitalized until November when he was posted as Commanding Officer of the Luftwaffe Fighter Leader School at Koenigsberg-Neumark, Germany, as part of General Adolf Galland's staff. In March 1945 when Soviet troops overran the base, Rall was reassigned to Jagdeschwader 300 as Kommodore where he flew the long-nosed Fw 190Ds. He remained with this unit until war's end operating from a base near Salzburg where he disbanded his unit in the face of advancing American troops in May 1945. He was captured by Allied forces and became a prisoner of war. He was shortly moved to Heilbronn and from there sent to England with other pilots who had at one time or another flew the Me 262. After much detailed questioning on the technical aspects of this aircraft and several others, Rall returned to Germany.

Rall ended the war with 275 enemy aircraft to his credit and ranks as Germany's and the war's third highest scoring fighter ace. He was shot down on five separate occasions himself, while flying in over 600 missions on attack or intercept roles. He was decorated with the Knights Cross on September 3, 1942, at which time his score stood at sixty-five, the Oak Leaves on October 26, 1942 and the Swords on September 12, 1943. The Me 109G flown by Rall as commander of III Gruppe JG 52 is illustrated on page 34.

In an effort to provide the Me 109G with more punch, a pair of 20mm cannon were installed in gondolas under the wings, but this configuration so hampered the aircraft's maneuverability, that pilots much preferred a single, engine mounted heavy weapon.

ROBERTS, Colonel Eugene P.
United States Army Air Force
(9 Victories)

Eugene Paul Roberts was born on September 12, 1917 in Wallace, Idaho, but considers Spokane, Washington, his hometown. In Spokane, Roberts attended Gonzaga High School where he graduated in June 1935. He then went to work for a year before returning to college at Gonzaga University in September 1936, graduating in June 1940.

Roberts joined the Army as a flying cadet immediately after graduation and was sent to Grand Central for assignment and then posted to Oxnard near Los Angeles, California, for his primary flight training. He was then returned to Grand Central for an additional six weeks in the Stearman PT-17, receiving his basic training at Randolph Field and his advanced training at Brooks and Kelly Fields, flying AT-9s. Roberts completed his flight training in February 1941 and was assigned to Hamilton Field, near San Francisco, California, as part of the 20th Fighter Group. Here he flew the Curtiss P-40 from February 1941 to February 1942 at which time he was transferred to the 14th Fighter Group which had been activated a year earlier at Hamilton. The unit split its squadrons up and actually flew from Hamilton, Oakland, California and San Diego, California for the remainder of the year.

In May 1942, Roberts was again transferred, this time to the newly activated 78th Fighter Group. Still stationed at Hamilton, he was given command of the 83rd Fighter Squadron. Then in July, Roberts was given command of the 84th Fighter Squadron and made base commander of the unit's station in Oakland.

Roberts went overseas with the 78th on November 24, 1942 leaving New York on the *Queen Elizabeth* and arriving in England on December 1st. The unit was assigned to Goxhill piloting P-38Gs. A month later, their P-38 aircraft were sent to Africa leaving Roberts and his three flight commanders at Goxhill to await the arrival of Republic P-47Cs from the United States. With the new planes came a new crop of pilots with a little over ten hours of flying time in the P-47. The 78th then moved to Duxford near Cambridge which was a permanent Royal Air Force installation.

Roberts flew his first operation on April 6th when he led his unit on a fighter sweep. The unit had not yet received their belly tanks and were limited in their radius of operations. Once the tanks arrived, the 78th was assigned to escort duty with Allied bombers and Roberts flew his first mission in this capacity on July 1st when he was credited with a probable Fw 190. During the next four months Roberts accounted for all his victories, achieving his first on July 30th when he destroyed a Fw 190 and two Me 109s. Following is a list of his victories and missions:

Date	Mission*	Victories
30 Jul 1943	87th	1 FW 190, 2 Me 109s
17 Aug 1943	106th	1 Me 110
24 Aug 1943	112th	1 FW 190, 1 Me 109
10 Oct 1943	153rd	1 Me 210, 1 Me 110
20 Oct 1943	163rd	1 Me 109

*Mission refers to 78th Fighter Squadron. Roberts did not participate in all missions.

In early 1944 Roberts was transferred to 8th Air Force Fighter Command Headquarters where he finished his first tour of duty with four more missions before taking a 30-day leave. On July 6th he returned to the 8th Air Force and was given command of A-3 operations for the 67th Fighter Wing where he stayed until December 31st at which time he was posted to command the 364th Fighter Group at Honington flying the North American P-51. Roberts reported on January 3, 1945 and during the remaining five months of the war flew over 110 hours in the Mustang, but was credited with only three probable victories (Fieseler Fi 156s) he had achieved during ground strafing operations.

Roberts flew over 89 separate missions with the 78th Fighter Group and another 27 with the 364th Fighter Group. In this time he had only one abort, that being a prop failure. The P-47C flown by Roberts as Commander of the 84th Fighter Squadron at Duxford during the summer months of 1943 is illustrated on page 63.

Roberts' *Spokane Chief*, a P-47D-10-RE. Eight .50 caliber machine guns. Speed: 433 mph. at 30,000 ft. Range: 640 miles clean at 350 mph. Ammunition capacity: 2200 rounds.

RÖDEL, Colonel Gustav
JG 27
Luftwaffe
(98 Victories)

Gustav Rödel was born in Merseberg, Germany on October 24, 1915. He enlisted in the Luftwaffe as a cadet in 1936 after graduating from high school. He won his wings in August 1936 and was commissioned on January 1, 1938. Rödel received advanced fighter tactics training until he was posted to Spain as part of the Luftwaffe's Condor Legion. After his return, he was assigned to JG 27 and scored his first victory on September 1, 1939 during the invasion of Poland. During the Battle of Britain he served as Staffelkapitän of 4/JG 27 and by 1941 was in full command of II/JG 27 as a Gruppe Kommandeur.

In the summer of 1943, with the transfer of Eduard Neumann (Kommodore of JG 27) to the Ministry of Defense in Berlin, Rödel was given command of JG 27. When he assumed command, JG 27 was comprised of three Gruppen of thirty-six aircraft each, but Rödel activated a fourth Gruppe and increased the size of each to forty-eight aircraft. He remained in this position throughout the North Africa campaign and the withdrawals to Tunis, Sicily, and Italy. In February 1945, Rödel was given command of the 2nd Fighter Division (2. Jagddivision) in Strade where his responsibilities included the day and night fighter air defense in North Germany, Schleswig-Holstein and Denmark.

Rödel was credited with a total of 98 enemy planes destroyed during his career which spanned the entire war. Of these 98 victories, 97 were achieved against the Western Allies, 52 of them while in North Africa. He completed over 1000 combat missions flying primarily in variations of the Me 109, and was decorated with the Knights Cross and Oak Leaves.

The Me 109E flown by Rödel as Grupperkommandeur of II/JG 27 and the Me 109G he piloted as JG 27 Kommodore are illustrated on page 44.

Best performing 109 was the F model, in terms of maneuverability and stability. This one was captured and repaired by the British for test evaluation.

SCHACK, Captain Guenther
JG 51
Luftwaffe
(174 Victories)

Guenther Schack, born in East Prussia, was the son of the Superintendent of the city of Elbing. He attended school in Elbing from April 1928 until his graduation during Easter week of 1938. Schack always dreamed of becoming a Luftwaffe pilot during his school years, but was turned down for service due to a knee injury he had suffered during a skiing accident. Dejected, he entered the Stuttgart Engineering College and from here went to the Aachen School of Mining, but at the outbreak of the war he again tried to enlist in the Luftwaffe and because of the personal intervention of Werner Moelders, was finally accepted. Following his flight training at Danzig and Stolp, Schack was assigned to Moelders' unit, JG 51.

Participating on the Russian Front, Schack as a member of III/JG 51 was one of the first Luftwaffe pilots to fly the Focke-Wulf 190A-4 fighter into combat. His first mission with the new plane occurred on December 17, 1942 when he was assigned escort duty to a formation of Ju 88 bombers. As the Luftwaffe flight approached the target area the unit was jumped by a flight of Soviet fighters, however, upon seeing the new German fighters they quickly broke off the engagement. On the return flight at an altitude of approximately 6500 feet, Schack came upon four Petliakov Pe-2s intent on strafing the JG 51 base. Schack and his wingman immediately turned to the attack and in quick succession destroyed two of the Russian fighter-bombers. The remaining Pe-2s began to break away and turn to the east with Schack in close pursuit. He followed the aircraft, firing at them alternately. Suddenly, both aircraft burst into flames and crashed. Schack and his wingman had, however, crossed over the Russian lines and had to head for home as their fuel was running low. Once the low flying pilots crossed into German territory, they spotted three more Pe-2s and estimating that both fuel and ammunition were adequate for one last pass, Schack set upon the Soviet aircraft. He was able to add one more to his day's total before the remaining planes broke off and over his own field there seemed to be no end to his "waggling" (the German fighter pilots' sign of victory). In his first flight with the Fw 190, Schack had accounted for no less than five Russian Pe-2s.

On January 29, 1943 Schack had another good day. Together with two other pilots from his Staffel, he was ordered to escort a Stuka flight against a Russian position along the front. After the target had been destroyed and Schack was forming up with the unit for the flight home, he received a radio communication that Russian bombers were attacking German positions near Novosil. As Schack's unit still had a good supply of fuel they decided to leave the Stukas and attack the Soviet Pe-8s. In a matter of five minutes all eight of the Soviet aircraft had been destroyed with Heindrich Dittlmann getting one, Karl-Heim Weber getting two and Schack the remaining five.

For the next two weeks Schack saw almost continuous combat and by February 11, 1943 had reached the 20 victory level. It seemed that every day he was returning from action and waggling his wings over the airfield. Schack's particular method of attacking was to fire out of a sweeping turn which took considerable skill in flying and marksmanship.

On February 23rd JG 51 had a highly successful day against the Soviet Air Force as Schack and Lt. Josef Jennewein, an Olympic skiing champion, each scored five victories. On one mission Schack attacked a tight formation of four Soviet fighters and destroyed three of them in a single pass. The following day bad weather set in over the Eastern Front and all flying was restricted for a one week period. This gave time to Schack and his staffel to rest, the first since the start of the Russian campaign the summer before.

On March 17, 1943 Schack achieved his 45th and 46th victories. Two weeks later JG 51's staff was moved to Brjansk and due to the short supply of the Fw 190, Schack's Staffel was re-equipped with the Me 109. Even without his favorite mount, Schack's score continued to rise and by August 1st he had accounted for his 60th kill. Six days later Schack's Gruppe was moved to Smolensk and their first sortie from their new base took off on the following day. Schack was up at 4:00 p.m. to escort bombers on a raid to Jelnja. During the mission, radio communication was received that low-level Russian aircraft were spotted near Jarzewo and Schack was sent to investigate. Along with his Staffel, which numbered only four planes, due to the attrition and availability of aircraft, Schack attacked the Soviet formation. He accounted for two of the enemy before he returned to the base for refueling and rearming. Schack took off again and with only two planes was ordered to escort another German bomber unit. At approximately 16,000 ft. over the target area the unit was attacked by two Soviet fighters which were quickly dispatched by Schack. He destroyed one and sent the other hurriedly home to its base of operations.

After returning to his base and rearming for a second time, Schack in command of a two plane flight took off for a third time being vectored to an incoming flight of 25 Russian Il-2s escorted by some 40 fighters. Schack accounted for two of the enemy before he returned to Smolensk for the final time that day.

The next day, August 9th, Schack accounted for his 70th victory although his own aircraft took hits from Russian cannon and machine guns. Four days later he completed his 500th mission, scored 4 victories to raise his total to 75, and was awarded the Gold Front Line Clasp (Battle Ribbon). On the same day, Karl-Heim Weber scored the Staffel's 100th kill.

On August 15, 1943 Schack and two young pilots of JG 51 were again ordered to escort Stukas on a dive bombing mission. After the target was hit the Luftwaffe formation was jumped by Soviet fighters and a dogfight ensued.

Scourge of Allied bomber streams was this Fw 190 A-5/U12 (Fifth Model of A series/12th modification.) It was one of two prototypes for the A-7/R-1, which carried a pair of 20mm cannon in each underwing tray, or one 30mm cannon in each tray. Both models carried an additional 20mm cannon in each wing root, giving the Fw 190 either six 20mm cannon or two 20mm weapons and two 30mm cannon, quite an arsenal for a fighter grossing under five tons.

Although his gunsight was faulty, Schack did accomplish the destruction of one of the enemy. Schack's two young companions had been busily engaged elsewhere in the fighting and did not see the action for confirmation so Schack sighting an anti-aircraft battery below at the border of Spas and Demenskoje dived down and waggled his wings inviting what he thought to be a German gun crew to witness his victory. The gun crew's answer came in the form of gunfire. Unknown to Schack, the Russians had already occupied the Demonskoje area. With a hole of over 20 inches in his left wing, the aircraft became very difficult to control, however, Schack found that by using his left knee as an aid he could hold the stick enough to keep the plane in a stabilized flight path. Since he was only at about 300 feet when his aircraft had been hit, he was very fortunate to be able to make it back to his base and land safely.

A short time later the unit moved to Brjansk where they joined II Gruppe of JG 54. The combined force then moved on to Gluchow in the Ukraine. At this time, Schack's Staffel had only a total of five pilots, including himself, and no planes in reserve.

On August 27, 1943 along with two other pilots from the 7th Staffel of III Gruppe, Schack was vectored to intercept a large Russian bomber formation escorted by over 30 Soviet fighters. Schack was successful in destroying one of the bombers before the three pilots, back in their familiar Fw 190s were attacked by the escorting fighters and forced to return home. The following day, Schack again narrowly escaped death when, during an encounter with Russian bombers, he was accidentally rammed by one of his own staffel while both were making passes at the same enemy fighter. Schack was able to retain control of his plane but his comrade crashed. With the third Fw 190 in the flight flying cover for him, he limped back to base and was able to make a successful crash landing.

On August 29th the 7th Staffel was transferred to Kontop and three days later Schack flew four separate missions. The action was so intense that after each of the four sorties, Schack was forced to make a belly landing. He scored his 100th victory on September 3rd and received personal congratulations from the Gruppe Kommandeur, but the time for celebration was cut short by the forced retreat to Trubschewsk on the Desna River, 62 miles south of their former base at Brjansk. On September 12, 1943 the unit again moved, this time to Poniatowka, west of Roslwal and then on the 15th retreated back to Smolensk. Although the retreat darkened Schack's feelings for the day, he was proud to celebrate JG 51's 7000 th victory.

On September 19th the unit was moved to Mogilew and on the 20th Schack scored his 109th victory. His unit switched airfields several times in the next few weeks before finally landing at Vitebsk on October 10th. Five days later Schack was given leave and went to Bad Wiesse in Bavaria. Upon his return on December 11, 1943, Schack found his unit had moved again to Bobruisk and that he had been assigned command of the 9th Staffel of III Gruppe JG 51, a fighter-bomber unit. Under his command, the 9th Staffel had fourteen pilots, seven of whom had tasted victory. There were Unteroffizer Gabriel Tautscher, with 57, Sergeant Kuken with 37, Lt. Venth with 8, Lt. Nebel with 8, Lt. Keisel with 6, Lt. Stickel with 6, and Sgt. Slomski with 2.

On the 15th Schack's Staffel was ordered to bomb the outskirts of a town with 550 lb containers, each holding a number of 5.5 lb splinter bombs. After making a successful attack, Schack noticed that his bomb was still on its rack and returned to make another approach on the target. As he made his second run he sighted four Soviet planes above him and, quickly pushing his bomb release, climbed with his wingman to meet the attackers. He caught the last of the four aircraft and within a few seconds shot it down. Only after seeing one of their comrades shot down did the other three planes make any effort to break their tight formation, but by then it was too late. Schack, with bombs still hanging from his rack, made his escape. He finally managed to jar the bomb loose over a swamp before landing at his base.

The weather turned bad for a short time during the end of December and into early January, but on January 10, 1944 Schack and his Staffel returned to combat flying. On the 16th Schack destroyed an Il-2 just east of Osaritschi, but was himself hit by Soviet fire and forced to bail out at some 250 mph in order to come down just inside the current German positions.

By the middle of February 1944, the unit had retreated back to Bobruisk again and in the beginning of March, III Gruppe finally got additional Fw 190s from I Gruppe which was reequipping with Me 109s. In the middle of March, Schack's Staffel was itself refitted with the Me 109 which did not make altogether good sense since the rest of the Gruppe had just received its Fw 190s.

Schack spent a short time longer with JG 51 before he was transferred to JG 3 where he served until the end of the war, finishing with 174 enemy aircraft to his credit and several awards, including the Knights Cross with Oak Leaves, awarded in April, 1944. The Folke-Wulf 190 A-4 Schack piloted as Staffel leader of the 9th Staffel of III Gruppe, JG 51 at Bobruisk, Russia in December 1943 is illustrated on page 48.

SCHILLING, Colonel David
62nd Fighter Squadron
56th Fighter Group
8th Air Force
(22.5 Victories)

David Carl Schilling was born on December 15, 1918 at Leavenworth, Kansas, and after graduating from high school attended Dartmouth College where he graduated in 1939 with a degree in geology. He enlisted in the Army Air Corps as a cadet and was sent to Lincoln, Nebraska for elementary training on August 14th. Schilling completed his basic instruction at Randolph Field, Texas and his advanced training at Kelly, where he graduated on May 11, 1940. He was posted to Langley Field, Virginia, but on November 11th was transferred to Mitchel Field in New York and assigned duty with the 8th Pursuit Group. From Mitchel Field, Schilling was sent to Charlotte, North Carolina to join the 56th Fighter Group as assistant Squadron Engineering Officer, a position he held until April 25, 1942. He then became Flight Commander of the 63rd Fighter Squadron, and on June 30th transferred to the 62nd Fighter Squadron in the same capacity. He commanded the 62nd in England from January 17, 1943 to August 20, 1943, was Executive Officer of the 56th Fighter Group until December 1st, Deputy Group Commander to August 13, 1944 and Group Commander to January 26, 1945 at which time he was appointed 65th Fighter Wing Operations Officer.

Schilling was credited with his first victories on October 2, 1943 when he destroyed a Me 109 and a Fw 190 over Emden, Germany, and reached ace status on October 10th when he downed another Fw 190 over Münster. On November 26, 1943 while on bomber escort duty, Schilling attacked a formation over Bremen, and destroyed two, while his unit was credited with a total of twenty-two without a single Allied loss. On April 9, 1944, again on escort duty, Schilling was credited with his twelfth and thirteenth victories, two Fw 190s. On December 23rd near Bonn, Schilling and his group attacked a formation of over 200 enemy planes and destroyed thirty-five of them with Schilling personally downing five. He ended the war with 22.5 enemy aircraft to his credit with an additional 10.5 ground victories and 10 damaged while flying over 350 combat hours.

Schilling was decorated with the Distinguished Flying Cross with eight clusters, the Silver Star with two clusters, the Distinguished Service Cross, the Air Medal with nineteen clusters and many awards from England and France. One of the P-47Ds flown by Schilling with the 56th Fighter Group is illustrated on page 40.

P-47C of the type flown by Colonel David Schilling while commander of the 62nd Fighter Sqdn. in 1943. C model was first to use water injection, permitting a war emergency rating of 2,300 hp. to be obtained at 27,000 ft.

STEINHOFF, Colonel Johannes
Luftwaffe
(176 Victories)

Johannes Steinhoff, born in Thuringia on September 15, 1913, enrolled at Jena University in 1932 to study languages, but in 1934 quit school to enlist in the German Navy for officers training. He transferred to the Luftwaffe in 1936 and by 1939 was a Staffel leader with 10/JG 26, a special night fighter unit of Me 109s. On December 18th, he scored one of this unit's first victories when he destroyed a RAF Wellington bomber attacking the German Naval base at Heligoland Bight on the North Sea. His staffel was incorporated into NJG 1, the first Night Fighter Wing, in late June 1940, under the command of Wolfgang Falck who quickly put Steinhoff in command of II Gruppe. Although the two men had become the best of friends during the early battles of the German Bight, Steinhoff asked and received a transfer to day fighters being posted to JG 52. He fought with this unit during the Battle of Britain and was later assigned with the unit to the Russian Front to command of II/JG 52. After several months, Steinhoff was transferred to JG 77 "Herzas", as Kommodore, in early 1943. He remained with this unit throughout the North African campaign and during the retreat to Sicily and Italy.

In December of 1944, after the death of Walter Nowotny, Steinhoff was put in command of the first operational jet unit, JG 7. However, in January 1945 a unique unit composed of aces, JV 44, was formed under the leadership of Adolf Galland, and Steinhoff was transferred to serve as second in command. On April 18th, he was taking off from Parchim with a full load of fuel and rockets when his landing gear collapsed after hitting a bomb crater and in the ensuing crash, Steinhoff was seriously burned. He spent two long years in hospitals undergoing plastic surgery and multiple skin grafts before he was finally released in 1947.

Johannes "Macky" Steinhoff was known as a true professional by those who flew with him, and was one of the few who flew from the beginning of the war until its end. He finished the war as the Luftwaffe's twenty-second ranked ace with 176 confirmed victories, six of which were attained with the Me 262, and was awarded the Knights Cross with Oak Leaves and Swords. One of the Me 109Fs flown by Steinhoff as Kommodore of JG 77 "Herzas" in Russia is illustrated on page 52.

Improved Daimler-Benz DB 605A with nitrous oxide injection, first appeared on the Me 109G-2, boosting the fighter to short bursts of over 400 mph at altitude. Armament was the same as on late Fs (one 20mm cannon in propeller hub, two rifle caliber cowl guns, later replaced by heavier 12.7mm weapons. Right: Cockpit of 109G, squared off frontal area shows how basic windscreen was beefed up over the years.

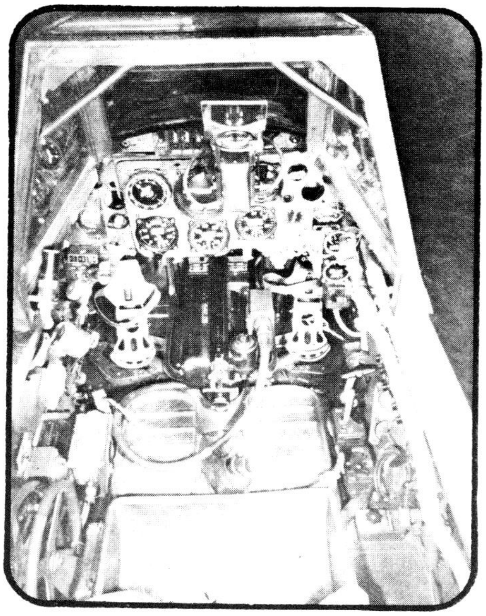

STEPHENS, Wing Commander Michael M.
229 Squadron
Royal Air Force
(22 Victories)

Michael Maurice Stephens was born in Ranchi, India on October 20, 1919, the youngest of three sons, all of whom served in the Royal Air Force, of a British Army Officer. His early years were spent in considerable moving, necessitated by his father's various military appointments. In January of 1936 he started work in the Port of London under a comprehensive training program for future senior executives, but Stephens decided he wished to make the Royal Air Force a career. Studying nights for the competitive entrance examination, Stephens passed this test and in September 1938 was accepted as a Flight Cadet in the Royal Air Force College, Cranwell.

Based on a normal training cycle, Stephens would have been scheduled to graduate in July 1940, but due to the increasing world tension and the possibility of war with Germany, his class was accelerated and he was commissioned in December 1939. By this time, Stephens had received approximately 100 hours in Avro Tutors and Hawker Harts. He was posted to No. 3 Fighter Squadron at Kenley, where he was given instruction in the Hawker Hurricane, this assignment lasting through the period of the so-called "Phony War".

On May 10, 1940 the German Blitzkrieg engulfed Belgium, Holland, and France, and Stephens' squadron was moved to Merville as part of the Air Component of the British Expeditionary Force. For the next few weeks, to the British evacuation of France, the squadron was heavily engaged against the continuous flights of Stukas, Heinkels, and both Me 109s and 110s. Stephens' first engagement with the Luftwaffe occurred on May 11th in the St. Trond area of Belgium and on this day, he destroyed two Ju 87s and a Do 17.

Stephens continued destroying Luftwaffe aircraft over the following two weeks, before the squadron was finally ordered home with advancing German forces just a few miles from their base. On May 14th he was credited with another Ju 87 and downed his first Me 109 to reach the status of "ace". He was promoted to a Flight Commander and on May 20th destroyed his second Do. 17.

Arriving back in England, No. 3 Squadron was transferred to the Northern sector where it remained operational, but was relatively inactive to allow the ground crews (who had been evacuated from Calais after taking part in the defense of the port) to recuperate, and also to train new pilots. During the Battle of Britain, because of this inactivity, Stephens was credited with only one additional victory, raising his total to eleven, and was decorated with the Distinguished Flying Cross and Bar.

In December 1940, he answered a call for volunteers to go to Greece, aboard the aircraft carrier HMS *Furious*. Stephens ended up in the Western Desert where he was assigned to 274 Squadron and participated in the retreat from El Agheila. From here he was posted to a Turkish Hurricane Regiment on the Bulgarian frontier, on a special assignment, for a short period before returning to the Western Desert in November, 1941, to take command of 80 Squadron equipped with Hurricane fighter-bombers.

On December 9th, while leading this squadron in attacks against German supply columns in the Tobruk area, Stephens was shot down. After completing a strafing run across the column, he looked up to find that a flight of Me 109s had joined the scene and were attacking his unit. Climbing to meet the threat, Stephens sighted one of his Hurricanes with a Me 109 on its tail and immediately turned toward the enemy plane. As he turned into the Luftwaffe fighter, another Me 109 pulled in behind him and opened fire. A cannon shell hit his starboard fuel tank while another exploded against the side of his cockpit. Wounded, Stephens pushed back the hood and started bail-out procedures just as the enemy plane flew by, but Stephens climbed back into his burning aircraft and lined up on the unsuspecting Luftwaffe pilot. He opened fire and watched as his shells danced across the fuselage of the Me 109. It rolled over, burst into flames and dove toward the earth below. At this point, the Hurricane became uncontrollable and Stephens finally bailed out, only to land within rifle range of the German lines, outside of Tobruk, which at this time was beseiged by enemy infantry and armor. He crawled as best he could toward Tobruk and in less than an hour was picked up by an Allied patrol and returned to friendly territory. For this action and those leading up to it, Stephens was decorated with the Distinguished Service Order.

Because of his injuries, Stephens was unfit for flying duty for several months, and was posted to RAF headquarters for the early part of 1942. He was then attached to the 57th Fighter Group, which had just arrived from the United States, until August 1942 when he was reassigned to command 229 Squadron on Malta. Heavily outnumbered by the combined German and Italian forces operating from bases on Sicily, the defenders of Malta had only five Spitfire squadrons with which to intercept the enemy and due to attrition, most of these had been reduced to an average of eight aircraft. During the first day of his new command, Stephens led the unit on two separate intercept operations and in the ensuing air battles was credited with an Italian Re. 2001. The following day, while again leading the squadron into action, he accounted for a Ju 88 and an Me 109. After sending the bomber into the Mediterranean Sea he was jumped by a flight of Luftwaffe fighters. Dropping to sea level and opening his throttle full he was able to keep ahead of his pursuers and on occasion would weave into the enemy planes in an effort to break up the chase. On one of these maneuvers, Stephens succeeded in flaming one of the Me 109s.

Stephens was made Wing Commander at Halfar, on Malta, and held this position until he returned to England in June 1943. During his tour he was credited with eleven additional enemy aircraft to raise his total to twenty-two and was awarded a second bar to his Distinguished Flying Cross.

In addition to the confirmed victories, Stephens was also credited with 18 probables.The Spitfire VB piloted by Stephens as Squadron Commander of 229 Squadron at Takali, Malta in early 1943 is illustrated on page 62.

A standard winged Spit IX is put through its paces.

STORRAR, Wng. Cmdr. James E.
239 Wing
Royal Air Force
(15 Victories)

Born June 24, 1921 in North Liverpool, Lancashire, England, James Eric Storrar, the "Kid Commander" left school at the age of seventeen and applied for a commisssion in the Royal Air Force in 1938. He commenced flight training at the DeHavilland School of Flying, piloting Tiger Moths and following this initial phase of training, was commissioned at Uxbridge and sent to No. 11 Flight Training School. Here, Storrar continued his training on Hawker Harts, Furys and Oxfords.

In September 1939 Storrar was posted to fly the Bristol Blenheim MK 1 (Fighter version) at Hendon, and in November he was transferred to form 145 Squadron at Croydon equipped with the Bristol Blenheim Night Fighter. In April 1940 the unit was reequipped with Hawker Hurricane Is. Early in May one flight from the Squadron was moved to Lille, France, for a few days following the German invasion, but was recalled to England and with the rest of the Squadron moved as a unit to Tangmere. From Tangmere, Storrar moved the unit forward each day toward the coast and finally arrived at Manston, near Dover, operating several hours each day over the beaches of Dunkirk in Northeast France. It was during this action that Storrar experienced his first taste of serious combat. On May 23rd, he destroyed a Me 110 for his first confirmed victory and the following day shared in the destruction of a Do 17. On May 27th he destroyed another Me 110 and in early June was credited with a He 111. In July, the Squadron was moved out of Tangmere to a small grass airstrip. It proved a worthwhile move for Storrar, as the day 145 Squadron left, Tangmere was bombed by Luftwaffe bomber formations.

Flying intercept missions against the incoming Luftwaffe bombers, Storrar continued to increase his score, and he ran up nine confirmed victories by the end of July. These included a Ju 88, two Me 109s, a Do. 17 and another He 111.

Although 145 Squadron scored an impressive victory ratio, the continued combat took its inevitable toll. (On the opening day of the Battle of Britain, the Squadron accounted for twenty-one German aircraft destroyed for the loss of only six pilots.) They had lost most of their pilots and all their serviceable aircraft and were therefore disbanded and reformed near Edinburgh, Scotland. After a few days rest the unit returned to action, but in early September Storrar was again transferred north of London to join 73 Squadron still flying the Hurricane I, from Debden. As the Battle of Britain died down, Storrar was transferred to 421 Flight (Jim Crow) at Gravesend flying Hurricane IIs specially lightened for high altitude interception. The aircraft had no pressure system and only primitive oxygen masks, even though they were expected to operate at between 30,000 and 40,000 feet.

As 73 Squadron was being posted to North Africa, Storrar returned to that unit in November embarking for the Western Desert on board the Carrier *Furious*. On arrival in West Africa, Storrar took off from the carrier with the rest of the unit and hopped between several small airstrips before finally landing at, first, Cairo and then Alexandria. From here it was just a short flight into the action of the Western Desert. On January 6, 1941 Storrar was credited with his first victory in the desert, destroying an Italian Fiat CR 42. This action came during the Allies push against the Italian Forces which carried as far as Benghazi. However, at this point, the Germans entered the conflict and the Squadron was forced to retreat along with other British units. Storrar was caught inside the fortress of Tobruk in April and here he achieved several additional victories including a Ju 87 on April 8th. After Tobruk was relieved, Storrar was sent to Test Flight duty and acted as Convoy Leader on the Trans-African route leading flights of Curtiss P-40 Tomahawks, Mohawks, and Kittyhawks to Cairo. On one occasion, during an unusually heavy rainy season, Storrar, and his flight, were forced to land in Siberia, near Moscovia, and was commended for getting everyone out safely.

In an unusual switch for a fighter pilot, Storrar then was posted to 208 Squadron flying the huge Sunderland Seaplane for a short while, before being sent home to England via Lisbon, Portugal. He then joined 55 Operation Training Unit as an instructor and was promoted to the rank of Squadron Leader. He was only twenty.

In January 1942 Storrar was sent to Central Gunnery School as a Fighter Leader, where he remained until December when he took command of 65 Squadron. During early 1943 the unit took a course on aircraft carrier deck landing, qualifying twelve pilots. This training was undertaken because of the possibility of 65 Squadron being used in the Mediterranean area to reinforce the Fleet Air Arm. After this training, however, the unit operated over France and the Low Countries on bomber escort and fighter sweep duty. Equipped with Spitfire IXs, Storrar's unit flew alongside many formations of American Fortresses and Marauders. In late 1943 the unit was reequipped with the Mustang III, however, Storrar was posted to Transport Command to form a unit called Air Delivery Letter Service. This unit was to deliver secret mail and documents by air to prevent radio message interception.

In creating this unit, Storrar was the first person to land and take-off from the Normandy beach after D-Day when, on June 9, 1944, he delivered secret mail to Allied commanders in his specially lightened Hurricane II.

Storrar was then reassigned, in yet another move, as a Wing Commander to lead a wing of three Mustang Squadrons chiefly responsible for long range escort and fighter strikes. He led this unit on anti-flak raids and commanded the fighter escort for the RAF Mosquito formation which attacked the Gestapo Headquarters in Copenhagen, Denmark. One of his last actions was the command of the fighter escort for the RAF Lancaster formation which bombed Hitler's "Eagles Nest" near Berchtesgaden, Bavaria.

Storrar ended the war in command of 239 Wing (Mustangs) in Northern Italy having been credited with fifteen confirmed aerial victories and having flown over 1120 operational hours, nearly all in single seat fighter aircraft, in four operational tours. He was decorated with the Distinguished Flying Cross and Bar and the Air Force Cross, and was, undoubtedly, one of the busiest pilots in the RAF. The modified two seat Mustang piloted by Storrar while Wing Commander of 239 Wing is illustrated on page 64.

Wing Commander James Storrar's P-51D (Mustang IV). Two hundred and eighty-one P-51Ds were delivered to the RAF. Together with 594 P-51Ks, they were known as Mustang IVs.

WALSH, Captain Kenneth A.
VMF-124
USMC
(21 Victory Credits)

Kenneth Walsh, born in Brooklyn, New York, on November 24, 1916, enlisted in the Marine Corps on December 15, 1933 and was assigned to Naval Flight Training at NAS Pensacola, Florida in March 1936 where he graduated in April 1937. For five years he served as an enlisted pilot (Naval Aviation Pilot) during which time he was assigned to observation and scout bomber squadrons until June 1941, when he fulfilled his ambition of being assigned to a fighter squadron. He was promoted to the rank of Marine Gunner (Warrant Officer) in May, commissioned as a 2nd Lt. in October, 1942, and was sent overseas as part of VMF-124 the following January. Between February and September 1943 Walsh operated from air strips in the Solomon Islands (Guadalcanal, the Russell Islands and Munda) and was credited with twenty of his twenty-one victories.

On March 3, 1943, Walsh entered into his logbook this laconic remark "Sunk 15-ton schooner (strafe) Vella Lavella." The coast watcher on Vella Lavella had reported being harassed by Japanese ground forces and had reported the recent arrival of a Japanese schooner which anchored in one of the lagoons located on the Northwest coast of the island area. With typical Australian reserve, he had reported the situation to Cactus (Guadalcanal) by wireless, and in effect, requested that the nuisance be taken care of. This information was relayed to Fighter Command and down to squadron level where Walsh was designated to lead a two plane flight and destroy the schooner. His wing man on this mission was Lt. William Bedford. Take off was at pre-dawn, and he followed a course south of the New Georgia Group of Islands at an altitude of 100 feet (to minimize detection by both enemy coast watchers and radar) until approaching the coast of Vella Lavella where he climbed to 10,000 feet. After some anxious moments, the schooner was located. Bedford spotted it first and Walsh promptly gave him the lead. As they commenced their attack it was noted that a small boat was tied along side which indicated that at least some personnel were aboard. It was just after sunrise and they apparently caught everyone by surprise. Walsh accomplished four strafing runs expending approximately 2000 rounds before departing the area. He left the main mast hanging in the water and the entire vessel smoking. The return flight proved uneventful and Walsh landed at Guadalcanal exactly three hours from the time he departed. Later in the day, the coast watcher expressed his appreciation for the assist, and reported that after the dead and wounded were removed, the vessel burned until it finally sank.

On April 1st Walsh was credited with his initial aerial victory, when he destroyed a Japanese Zero near the Russell Islands, and by May he had reached ace status. He was credited with multi-victory days on April 1st, May 13th, August 15th and August 30th. For his actions on the latter two dates, Walsh was awarded the Congressional Medal of Honor. On the 15th, he repeatedly dove his Corsair into an enemy formation out-numbering his own division by 6 to 1, and destroyed two dive bombers and one fighter, even though his aircraft was hit numerous times. On the 30th, Walsh was escorting a formation of B-24 bombers for a raid on Kahili Air Base, Bougainville, where he encountered a formation of over 50 enemy fighters. He attacked and downed four of the enemy before he was forced to crash land near Vella Lavella. These four victories were his seventeenth through twentieth.

Walsh returned to the States after completion of his first tour, but was back in action with VMF-222 in April 1945. Between April and June he operated from Samar, Philippines where he employed his F4U in a fighter-bomber capacity. Walsh was credited with his final victory on June 22nd when he downed a Kamikaze (Zero). From June to September 1945 he was based at Okinawa. He flew over 140 combat missions and, in addition to the Congressional Medal of Honor, was decorated with the Distinguished Flying Cross and the Air Medal. He finished the war as the fourth ranked Marine ace and was the first pilot to reach ace status in the Corsair. The F4U-1 flown by Walsh prior to the action of August 30, 1943 is illustrated on page 57, and is the aircraft in which he destroyed twenty enemy planes.

The last Corsair to see action in WW II, the Vought F4U-4, flying with the 2nd Marine Air Wing, Death Rattlers Sqdn. over Okinawa. With 170 lbs. of armor plate in cockpit, alone, F4U-4 was extremely tough machine to bring down.

WOLFRUM, Lieutenant Walter
JG 52
Luftwaffe
(135 Victories)

Walter Wolfrum, born in Northern Bavaria on May 23, 1923, finished his schooling at Nuremberg before enlisting in the Luftwaffe in October, 1940. In March, 1941, he began his flight training at Luftkriegsschule II (Air-war School) at Berlin/Gatow, graduated as a fighter pilot in January 1943, and was assigned to II/JG 52 in Southern Russia, immediately after the German disaster at Stalingrad.

As a member of the 5th Staffel, Wolfrum flew his first combat sorties over the Kuban bridgehead. However, he met with little success as far as aerial combat was concerned, being twice wounded before he achieved his first credited victory, a Yak-1 fighter near Krymskaya, on his 60th mission. His second through sixth victories included a MIG-1, a YAK-1, and four Il-2 ground attack aircraft. These planes were destroyed over the great tank battle at the Mius River east of Stalino in July 1943. From this time on, after his 150th mission, Wolfrum considered himself a competent veteran combat pilot, and after a leave during the winter of 1943/1944 proved his point.

On March 25th 1944 he was credited with destroying six Soviet aircraft. In the morning he shot down two Lagg-3 fighters over the straits of Kertch (Crimea) and followed this with a Douglas Boston bomber and three Il-2s in the afternoon while protecting a German ship convoy near Eupatoria.

In April, 1944, the Soviet Army's offensive against the German held positions in the Crimea area of Russia, found Wolfrum based with II/JG 52 at the fortress of Sevastopol. On the 15th, Wolfrum was shot down defending this position. It occurred just after he had destroyed his 69th and 70th aircraft (two Il-2s) east of the city. Unable to open his canopy after being hit, he decided to try an emergency belly landing between German anti-aircraft batteries on a hill overlooking Sevastopol. Seconds after the touchdown of the plane, it exploded and Wolfrum suffered severe burns on his head, legs and arms.

Pulled from the aircraft, Wolfrum was transferred from the field hospital at Sevastopol to Rumania for extended recuperaton, before returning to combat.

After his recovery, Wolfrum became the Staffelkapitän of the 1st Staffel (I Gruppe) of JG 52 located on the Bessarabian Front in the north of Rumania. In the following months Wolfrum was to achieve his greatest successes of the war. Within three days, the 30th of May to the 1st of June 1944, he was credited with 21 confirmed victories in the Battle of Jassy. Eleven of these came in one day, May 30th, and his actions were included in the Wehmachtabericht (German Forces Report). Seventeen of these 21 planes destroyed by Wolfrum were American lend-lease Bell P-39 Aircobras.

Fighting with the 1st Staffel against the Russian offensive West of Lemberg (Galicia) Wolfrum increased his score to 126 by July 16th. This achievement was reached with four victories on July 15th and ten more on the 16th. However, on July 16th, after his 10th victory of the day, Wolfrum was seriously injured when a half-inch shell exploded in his cockpit, piercing his abdomen and pelvis.

Fighting the excruciating pain, Wolfrum was able to return to his base, and in a matter of two hours was lying on the operating table in a hospital at Lemberg. For his actions of the 15th and 16th, Wolfrum was recommended for the Oak Leaves to his Knights Cross and again was mentioned in the German Forces Report.

After a stay of six months in several German hospitals, Wolfrum returned to service in February 1945 when he took over his old Staffel in Silesia, Czechoslovakia. (Not one pilot who had flown with him in 1944 remained with the unit as attrition and transfer had taken its toll.) Continuing to add to his own score, Wolfrum was again shot down twice by Yak-9s over Breslau, during sorties when his meager unit was often outnumbered 20 to 1.

Wolfrum ended the war on May 8, 1945, when he surrendered along with the other pilots and personnel of I/JG 52 to American forces at Pisek, Czechoslovakia. He was turned over to Soviet troops, but released six weeks later due to the severe wounds he had suffered just prior to the surrender.

He was credited with a total of 137 confirmed aerial victories during his combat tours with JG 52 and was decorated with the Knights Cross. The Me 109 G-6 flown by Wolfrum with the 5th Staffel of II Gruppe is illustrated on page 53.

Wolfrum's favorite aircraft, the Me 109F. With two small cowl guns and either one 30mm or one 20mm cannon firing through the propeller hub, it was the best German dogfighter of the war.

YASUDA, Warrant Officer Yoshito
Japanese Army Air Force
(10 Victories)

Yoshito Yasuda, born on July 4, 1916 in 3otsu City, Japan, enlisted in the apanese Army Air Force in December 1936 and after completion of his basic raining was assigned to the 6th Sentai in Korea as a ground equipment crewman. He was later transferred to the ndependent 9th Chutai (a small force lesigned to be mobile for quick dispersement, and operating ndependently of the regular Japanese Army Air Force Command) where he served during the Japanese-Sino War of 1937 from bases in Northern China. In August, 1938, a reorganization assigned Yasuda to the 3rd Chutai of the 64th Sentai where he remained for a year before he was admitted to the Klimagaya Army Air Flying School. Yasuda completed his flight training in July, 1940 and returned to the 64th which was now based in Manchuria.

In August 1941 the 64th, which had moved to Canton, China, received the new Nakajima Ki-43 and the transition rom their older model aircraft took until November to complete. On December 4th, Yasuda and the 64th were moved to du Phu Quoc, a small island off the Cambodian coast and three days later were flying escort duty over Japanese roop convoys. On December 10th the 64th moved forward to a base at Kota Bharu and for the next several weeks ook part in the methodical destruction of British air power in the Malaya area. Yasuda experienced his first aerial combat on December 22nd when eighteen Hayabusas of the 64th encountered a formation of fourteen British Buffaloes. Yasuda was serving as wingman for the Commander of the 3rd Chutai, Captain Yasuma, and although he did not score, he did gain valuable experience that would benefit him in the months to come.

As the new year began, Yasuda and the 64th moved from Kota Bharu to Ipoh, where, between the 12th and the 31st, they carried out continuous attacks on the British airfield at Singapore. During this time Yasuda was credited with his first victories of the war when he shot down two Royal Air Force Hurricanes. On February 6th, Yasuda participated with the 64th in the attacks on the Dutch airfield at Palembang, Sumatra, in preparation for a Japanese air drop on the oil refineries in the area. The following day the 64th went back to Palembang, and while the 1st and 2nd Chutai flew top cover, Yasuda and the 3rd Chutai strafed the field destroying ten planes and damaging six. After completing his ground run Yasuda climbed to join the aerial fight and was credited with sharing in the destruction of a Hurricane with two other pilots of the 64th. Finally on February 14th, the airborne operation was attempted with the 64th flying cover. The paratroopers successfully secured the base the following day and the 64th moved to Palembang on the 18th. The following day they mounted an attack on Djakarta and Bandung in Western Java where Yasuda engaged in aerial fights with both Curtiss 75A Hawks and Boeing B-17s. He was credited with one victory for the day, while the 64th totaled twelve.

Following the Java operation, the unit moved to Chiang Mai, Thailand and from here flew attacks against Burma. Here Yasuda's opposition were the "Flying Tigers" of Chennault. On April 8th the 64th took off to attack Loi Wing. They

strafed the field destroying several enemy planes, but then were jumped from above by a formation of over twenty P-40s. The 64th suffered heavy losses with four of its finest and most experienced pilots being killed, among them Captain Yasuma (Yasuda's C.O.) and Sgt. Haruto Wada. The following day the 64th returned to Loi Wing and Yasuda was credited with the

Remains of an early Ki.43, of the type flown by Yasuda against the A.V.G. Flying Tigers early in 1942. Oscar replaced fixed gear Ki. 27 Nate which opened the war in Burma in 1941. Gun ports for pair of 12.7mm machine guns show clearly. They were nearly useless against head on diving attacks by American flown P-40s, but far more effective than Nate's twin 7.7mm machine guns, which barely chipped the P-40s paint. To survive in combat against the heavily armed Americans, pilots like Yasuda relied on their aircraft's agility and many years of aerobatic training.

destruction of a Curtiss P-40, in a dog-fight, as well as several others on the ground. On April 26th Yasuda and the unit were again on escort duty with a formation of paratroop transport aircraft when bad weather developed and the scheduled drop was cancelled. Yasuda developed a fuel leak in his Hayabusa and was forced to leave the returning formation. As the weather closed in on him, the leak grew worse and, finally, Yasuda decided to crash land. It took him four days to navigate from behind the Allied lines, but on the 30th he finally arrived back with the 64th ready to get back in action. During the month of May, the 64th was assigned to duty of interception over Akyab. Day after day, flights would take off one after another. On one of these missions, Yasuda shot down a Lockheed Hudson.

As the monsoon began in June, the 64th retired to Mingaladon where combat activity was very limited due to the weather. The unit carried out a few training sorties through August before returning to Japan to equip with new Ki-43s. They returned to Singapore in September. On November 23rd Yasuda and Captain Kuroe took off from Mingaladon to intercept a flight of B-24s attempting to reach their base. Yasuda picked out one of the enemy bombers and attacked, but as he completed his pass, his aircraft was hit by the enemy fire and burst into flames. Yasuda suffered severe facial burns, but managed to parachute to safety. He was credited with a share of the victory.

As the year 1942 came to a close, Yasuda and the 64th were equipped with the newer Ki 43 II. They returned to Burma from Japan in the middle of February and immediately were assigned to ground support duty for the Japanese forces around Akyab. By March, Yasuda and the 64th began to feel the strength of Allied air power. In Yasuda's own words: "Three commanders plus many good pilots had been killed in action. In spite of our victories, the enemy's air power was increased, and we felt hardship in defense. All but four of the pilots I had flown with since 1941 had been killed."

Then in July, 1943, Yasuda was transferred to the Klimagaya Army Air Training School as an instructor where he remained until May 1945 at which time he was posted to the 246th Sentai and assigned to defend Osaka, Kobe, and Kyoto. Yasuda claimed his final victory with this unit when he destroyed a North American P-51 during a dogfight over Biwako Lake on August 14, 1945. He ended the war with 10 victories and over 3500 hours in the air. The Nakajima Ki-43 flown by Yasuda with the 64th Sentai early in 1943 is illustrated on page 55.

Flying the Royal Air Force Westland Whirlwind

by Group Captain Arthur H. Donaldson, DSO, DFC, AFC, RAF, Ret.

The design of the Whirlwind started in 1935 in response to Air Ministry Specification F .37/35 under the direction of W.E. Petter, Chief Designer for the Westland Aeroplane Company. (Mr. Petter also designed the Canberra Bomber, the Lighting Fighter, currently RAF Fighter Command's front line defense, and the Folland Gnat, the RAF's present trainer.) The low wing, twin engine monoplane was of all metal construction with stressed-skin covering. It was just over 32 ft. in overall length and had a wing span of 45 ft. Overall empty aircraft weight was 8300 lbs, while the loaded weight varied between 10,000 and 11,000 lbs, depending on the mission and weapon stores carried.

Test flown in October 1938, the first orders from the Air Ministry were placed for 200 Whirlwinds in January 1939. It entered RAF service in June 1940 when the initial deliveries were made to 25 Squadron at North Weald, but these planes were shortly after reassigned to 263 Squadron at Drem. Due to production delays of the engines, full squadron strength was not reached until early 1941.

Although basically designed as an interceptor fighter, the Whirlwind arrived in service at the same time as the later modified versions of the Supermarine Spitfire. As an interceptor fighter, its performance was very similar to the Spitfire, though it could not quite reach the same altitude, and having twin engines it could not compete with the Spitfire from an economic standpoint.

However, the Whirlwind had one vital asset which, at that time, no other aircraft possessed; its armament consisted of no less than four 20mm cannons fixed in its nose and firing forward. This armament was superior to any other aircraft in the fighter role (the Hurricane and Spitfire started with .303 caliber guns, though the later Spitfire had two 20mm cannons fitted). In addition, the Whirlwind could carry two 500 lb bombs under the wings. Thus, the Air Ministry realized that its true value was as a Ground Attack Fighter or Fighter Bomber.

The Whirlwind had excellent one engine performance, though it was a little handicapped in this respect in tha each engine had its own fuel supply system so that in the event of engine failure, it was impossible to use the fuel from the tank of the dead engine on the remaining live engine.

It was a very robust aircraft. On one occasion I was shot up by ground flak, 40mm Bofors type. My helmet was torn from my head and I received head injuries; the cockpit canopy was smashed and there were over 100 holes in the aircraft, yet it brought me safely home across 120 miles of sea, although I had to land with my undercarriage up because it was too damaged to let down.

The speed of the Whirlwind was similar to the Spitfire and the Luftwaffe's Fw 190. It was certainly as maneuverable as the 190, and probably more so. I can remember being attacked from the rear by a Fw 190, which I had no difficulty in shaking off by turning steeply.

Another advantage enjoyed by the Whirlwind over most other fighters were the slats fitting to the leading edge of both wings. These came out at slow speeds thus increasing the lift and reducing the stalling speed. The aircraft was therefore able to land in a much shorter space than most fighter aircraft of that period. The obvious advantage in a dog fight was that as soon as one pulled back hard on the stick, the slats came out and one could tighten the offensive or evasive turn even more.

The Whirlwind had two Rolls-Royce Peregrine 12-cylinder liquid-cooled engines, each developing 850 hp. Westland could have fitted a more powerful engine and improved the performance of the Whirlwind, but by then the jet engine had been invented and the Gloster Meteor fighter was entering service, so that the cost was considered prohibitive.

All in all, I can honestly say that I consider the Whirlwind to be the finest plane I have flown, and I must have flown over 100 different types, both British and American. The Spitfire was nicer in some respects, but the fact that the Whirlwind had two engines made one feel very safe, especially when one had been hit over enemy territory.

A Comparison of the North American P-51 and the Lockheed P-38

by Brigadier General Robin Olds, USAF, Ret.

Though seldom admitted by ardent supporters (particularly during bar flying sessions so loved by all fighter jocks) every fighter aircraft has its weaknesses and idiosyncrasies. Naturally, these are exploited to the full in all arguments and the verbal bombast comparing the good points of one versus the bad points of the other most often leave the participants in a total state of rage and frustration. It scarcely matters that neither man has flown the aircraft which he denounces so positively; rumor and heresay serve adequately to render all points of contention technically flawless; unbiased, and irrefutable. Sweet reason, a sense of justice and fair play, Robert's Rules of Order, and "equal time" has no application in this favorite pastime. Nor should they, for the relationship between the pilot and his fighter aircraft is a matter of deep emotion, and everyone knows that love is blind.

However, there are a goodly number of old tigers who flew two types in the same conflict, or who have flown several types in three conflicts, and their wisdom is the knowledge of Job. In the natural order of things, their participation in the passionate verbal battles is not just unwelcome, but downright resented. So in the main, the older warrior listens with amused tolerance, occasionally keeps the pot boiling, and takes full advantage of every roll of the dice to replenish his glass at the expense of the others.

In comparing the P-51 and the P-38 in combat, I make concession to no one nor give consideration to any, save the reminder that my impressions are based upon a particular theatre (ETO) at a particular time (1944-1945) and in no way imply a broader consideration of operational circumstances at other places or other times.

The P-38 was a wonderful fighter in many respects, and having been weaned on it, I loved it, up to a point. It was fast, easy to fly (once you really knew it), and would turn with the best of them; provided you had an exceedingly strong right arm. It was honest in most respects, giving ample stall warning under all flight conditions, and easy to recover if you ignored it. With proper power management, it had fine endurance and could cover the bombers all the way in and out again, or carry its own bombs and guns deep into Germany. Its four .50 caliber machine guns and its single 20mm gave it good fire power. It was acceptably rugged and could absorb a respectable beating and still get you home. Yet for the ETO, the old Lightning suffered some critical disadvantages, many of which reduced its overall effectiveness. Take the matter of creature comfort. Cockpit heating was practically ineffectual and prolonged exposure at high altitude in those climates were nothing short of agony. Bulky flying clothing was essential, and added to the misery of any pilot of my stature in that cramped cockpit. I had to sit with my neck bent forward hours on end, feet and hands aching with the cold, unable in any way to stretch or turn for relief. Cockpit visibility was poor by fighter standards. The bulk of the two engine nacelles hid a large part of each horizon and the mass of the wing hid anything behind and below you. Control of fuel flow from the various tanks was a nightmare of illogical design and demanded constant attention. While every other instrument or engine control was arranged in a logical pattern of *Left-Right*, the fuel selector valves (hidden on the floor to the left of the seat) were *Right-Left* — a constant source of potential error.

Apparently the turbo superchargers were next to impossible to trim during ground maintenance for, at altitude, the pilot, more often than not, got too much boost from one and not enough from the other. This took a lot of attention to engine gauges and forced you to fly with a wide divergence in throttle settings, an uncomfortable requirement at best.

While the redundancy of two engines seemed a blessing, and I came home many times with one feathered, I can't help reflecting that I came home *all* the time on one engine in the P-51! In addition, the P-38 didn't like to fly on one engine with the gear down. This made engine loss on take off a real adventure, if not a disaster. The same applied to getting the gear down when you had lost hydraulic power and were on a single engine. The hand pump provided for this contingency was wonderfully inefficient. Interminable pumping against ever-increasing resistance made the task almost impossible, unless you started at a great height and completed the task before you ran out of altitude.

Many will remember the unique plan view and profile of the P-38. It could be seen and recognized for miles by any viewer. I always felt the Luftwaffe delighted in this characteristic for it gave them the choice to engage or disengage at will. By the same token, one would have expected the B-17 gunners to recognize the P-38 as a friend with the same ease. Perhaps they did, but they shot at you just the same, a matter of conditioned reflex, I suppose.

In spite of all this, the P-38 was a good air-to-air fighting machine. The one glaring defect that kept it from being superior in air combat was the unalterable and ever-present aerodynamic fact that once pointed down in any prolonged dive, it would continue in that direction regardless of what you, Lockheed, Allison, or any other responsible authority wanted to do about it. The phenomenon is well understood today. In those days, the aerodynamic effects of compressibility were something of a mystery. The P-38 acted like a horse with the bit in its teeth. Pull back on the yoke, and it bowed its neck and dove even steeper. Only a terrifying descent to denser air provided any hope of solution, and that depended on pilot skill, time and remaining altitude. While we didn't fully understand this, we knew full well that it would happen — and so did the German pilots. I can remember the many times I had to watch with impotent rage while a Me 109 or Fw 190 split s'd away from a fight at altitude. We were more than eager to make the change at the time our group converted to P-51s.

Much as we liked the P-38, we knew what the "Spam Can" could do and we wanted a piece of the action. For the pilots who had never flown a single engine fighter, the conversion was something of a minor trauma. This little beauty had torque a-plenty, and we quickly found it necessary to convert our strong right arms to strong right legs. We also learned that the most important control, aside from stick and rudders, was the rudder trim knob. It also took a bit of self-hypnosis to ignore the peculiar sounds the Merlin engine always made the moment you flew over any stretch of water.

In addition, it was weeks before any of us became even the slightest bit accustomed to the soul-shattering thump that occurred each time we climbed or descended through the altitude where the supercharger blower cut in or out. This is not to mention the sheer panic the first time you ran a drop tank dry deep over Germany and the

Text continued on page 108

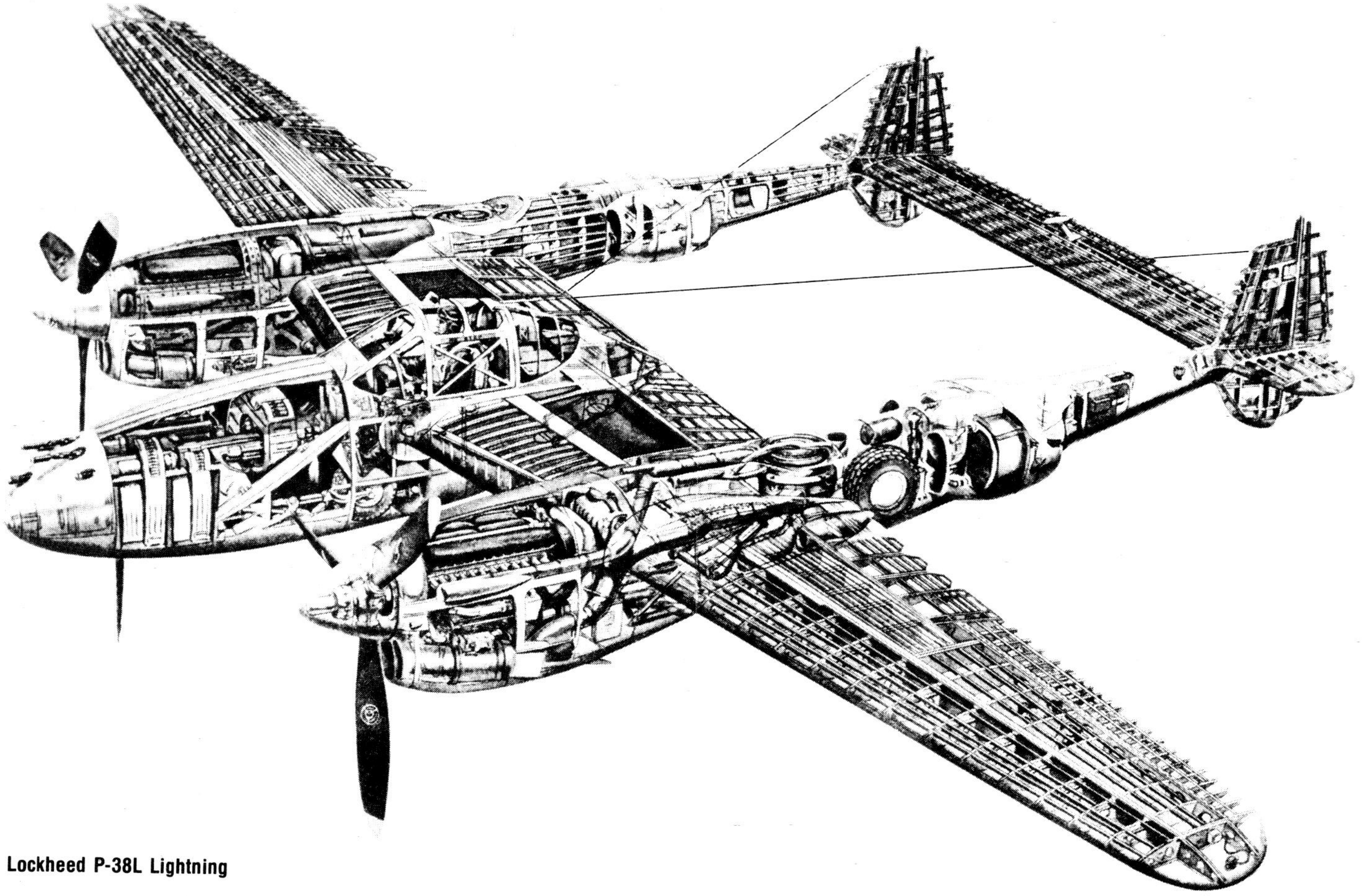

Lockheed P-38L Lightning

"The Flying Undertaker", a North American F6K Mustang, photo-recon version of the P-51D. Flown by Captain William A. Shomo, of the 82nd Tactical Reconnaissance Sqdn, who shot down seven Japanese aircraft in an aerial melee over the Philippines, on January 11, 1945, it helped provide Shomo with the highest single mission score for a U.S. fighter pilot during WW II. On that same mission Shomo's wingman, Lt. Paul Lipscomb, shot down three of the enemy. The entire fight took only 12 minutes. During that time, Shomo flamed six Tonys and a Betty Bomber, while Lipscomb was shooting down two Tonys and a Tojo fighter.

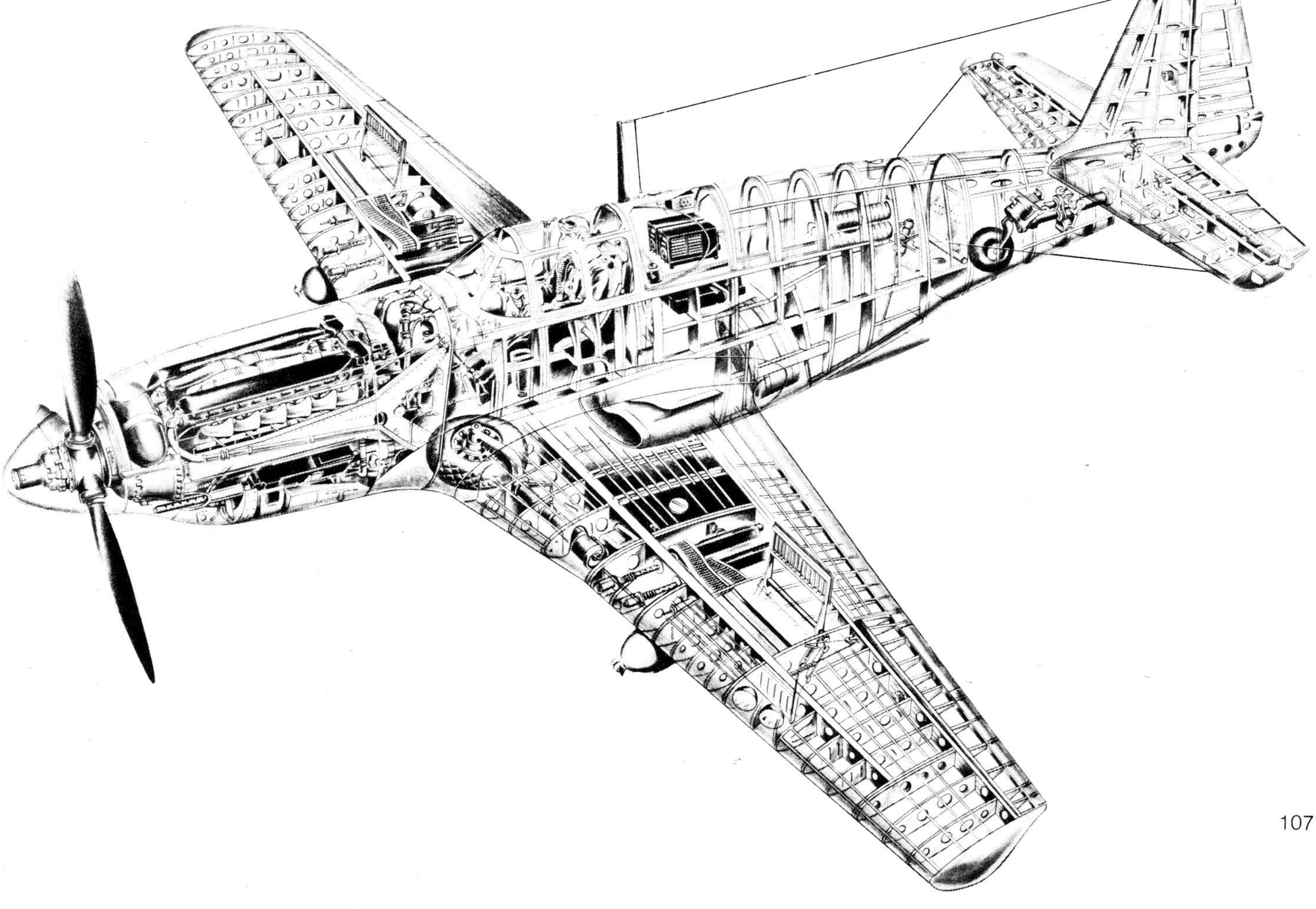

engine cut out instantly. But the joy of flying that absolutely fabulous little machine far out-matched any of its annoying little habits. At last we sat in comfort, plenty of room for legs, arms, shoulders, and head, ample heat at any altitude, fantastic pilot visibility all around (except over the nose of course — and who cared what was in front) and a range capability we hadn't dreamed of. There were a few minor annoyances of course. Center-of-gravity (C.G.) was crucial with the fuselage tank filled. But we learned to cope. Trim was critical if you wanted to hit anything with those six wing-mounted fifties — but that was what the rudder trim was for and you learned to use it. Landing was sporty, but you soon took pride in placing the bird gently on the runway in a three-point attitude. Even taxiing in a constant "S" turn to afford forward visiblity either side of that long engine cowling became a matter of routine habit.

The ultimate proof and moment of truth came in your first air combat. Here was a fighter! High or low, straight down, or in a shuddering Lufberry you knew no one could match you. The gyro sight was deadly accurate. The firepower devastating. Gun camera results were like Hollywood, a far cry from the blurred, jumping imagery produced by the gun camera in the P-38 (some knothead had mounted that one right under the 20mm gun).

As for actual combat performance of the two aircraft, let me state briefly that the P-38 below about 15,000 feet would out turn any German fighter. It wasn't easy and many of our pilots couldn't do it, but it was a fact. I did it and others did it. Also, the P-38 was as fast as anything else on the deck in a flat out chase (except perhaps the British Tempest and the long nosed Fw-190). The P-51 was good at everything, matching the German machines in all they could do. Some argue that one or the other had an advantage, given equal pilots — I don't know. I never met an equal pilot in a Fw-190. I met a *better* one once and felt lucky to get home in one piece.

In all, the P-51 was a fighter pilot's dream, and today remains one of the two best machines I have ever flown. If you don't think I'm right, just ask any pilot who ever strapped a Mustang to his bottom and set out across the North Sea to do battle with the wily Hun.

Royal Air Force Supermarine Spitfire

by Group Captain Michael M. Stephens, DSO, DFC, RAF, Ret.

I consider that the most agreeable aircraft I've flown, from a sheer flying and handling viewpoint, was the clipped wing Spitfire V. The later marks, such as the IX, XII, and XIV were magnificent aircraft, with all the power one could demand; but for me they were not the same delight from a handling and aerobatic standpoint.

Having said this, I must add that when I was in Malta during 1942 and 1943 flying the Spitfire V, we all felt the need for the later and more powerful marks. The German and Italian Forces were flying Messerschmitt 109Fs and Gs, and almost invariably had the drop on us. They were able to exploit their superiority in climb and dive, come in well above us, swoop down for a quick shot, and climb away again. This gave them the initiative most of the time. One used to watch them above, watch them begin their dive, and hold steady until they were reaching firing range, and then break violently into the attack, usually following this manoeuvre with a half roll and pull-out, hoping to catch them in the dive, as they were already traveling considerably faster than us, and their diving speed was greatly superior, but sometimes, by cutting the corners, one was able to catch them pulling up for their next attack.

We found that the Italians were much more inclined than the Germans to "mix-it", they threw their aircraft around with great abandon (which was often a mistake). In a dog fight we could always out-manouevre them, whereas the Germans exploited their climb and dive superiority, which made it hard to catch them.

If only we had been equipped with the Spitfire IX during the difficult times in the autumn of 1942, the score boards would have looked very different!

Part of the problem, in fact the major problem, was that it was a major operation for us to get new aircraft int Malta. You will find, for example, that most of the Spitfires brought in, regardless of expense, in August 1942, were destroyed on the ground immediately after they had landed, having been flown off the carriers. The were caught before they had time to refuel. The Germans, on the other hand had no problem in replacing the aircraf they lost. New 109s were flown straigh down from Germany without loss or hindrance.

Also, our Spitfires were "tropicalized", that is they had the enlarged air cleaners fitted. This was essential to conserve engine life, which again was dictated by the difficulty of replacing worn-out aircraft. These air cleaners reduced the performance of th aircraft even further. The Germans had no worries on this score, for as I have mentioned, their replacement problem was infinitely easier.

What was the most difficult aircraft t shoot down? Without any hesitation, I can say that the one which I found the hardest was the Henschel 126! If he saw you coming (and his life depended on his doing so) he could turn on a dime, and if it was well-flown, could almost invariably keep the game up until the Spitfire, or Hurricane, finally had to break it off. I had several inconclusive engagements with these aircraft. They may have been frightened to death, but didn't get them.*

*In 1942 the obsolete Henschel 126 high wing monoplane, which had long been relegated to flying schools was pressed into service in the Balkans and Southern Europe for observation and partisan harrassment duties. In these roles it was flown by ex-flying instructors, all of them crack pilots.

AG

P

D